BUILDING BRIDGES

MADE ON PURPOSE
FOR A PURPOSE

Keep Calm + Build a Bridge!

Steph Fink

STEPH FINK

D1166984

Xulon
PRESS

It's not build a bridge and get over it; it's build a bridge and get to it – the precious hearts who need to know God loves them. Go build and tell them the good news! Steph Fink

TABLE OF CONTENTS

Dedication vii

Acknowledgements ix

Preface xiii

Chapter 1 – Keep Calm and Build a Bridge 17

God is alive and wants to use you!

Chapter 2 – If I Only Knew Then What

I Know Now 29

Judging is God's job; loving is our job.

Chapter 3 – Lead With Love 44

People are hurting and need their pain

acknowledged, not overlooked.

Chapter 4 – In AND Out 68

Life-changing ministry occurs both inside

and outside church building walls.

Chapter 5 – Unleashed 83

Forgiveness changes hearts.

Chapter 6 – The Gap 104

>We all have gaps, every last one of us.

Chapter 7 – Go is in the Gospel. 133

>God made you on purpose for a purpose. Go and
>make more disciples.

Additional Resources for Further Reading . . . 157

Notes 159

DEDICATION

I dedicate this book to my father, Peter Karl.
I miss you so much, Pop. Thank you for
teaching me to, "Keep punching!" because
it's helped me, you've helped me, finish
this book and continue purposefully living
this great life I've been gifted. #teampop

ACKNOWLEDGEMENTS

I first want to thank the Builder and the Author of all hope, Jesus. You've changed my life. Thank you for loving me, never giving up on me, and relentlessly building bridges to me.

My wonderful, patient and incredibly loving one and only, the Finkster. I am utterly crazy about your fine 80's self. Thank you for believing in me and being there, from listening to editing changes to emptying dishwashers to "encouraging" our offspring to, "let Mom work!" to needed hugs. You showed up and I'm so grateful to call you mine, forever.

My parents, Gwen and Peter Karl. Mom, your Bible remains my greatest bridge to your heart and Pop, your stubborn "keep punching" determination encourages me daily as does the drink coffee daily gene you passed me. You could have kept the thick-calved gene to yourself, though.

My pastors, David and Jo Ann Baird, for faithfully leading, preaching, living and endorsing a bridge building community in our The Life Church DC church family whose impact far exceeds our church building walls.

My friends, Carolyn and Pastor Phil Holliday, for their encouragement, friendship and wisdom during a critical bridge building time. So much of this book's essence was formed in the boardroom years ago through your pioneering spirits, love and leadership.

My friends who stood in the gap when I stepped far from my comfort zone to build different bridges. Your timely words of encouragement, prayers, bible verses and friendship gave and gives me courage to keep building: Karly Beckwith, Liz "Laverne" Carroll, Beth Davidson, Lynn DiGiovine, Dr. Ivonne Ellison, Colleen "Bon Qui Qui" Forsythe, David Fink, Laura "Mother Nature" Gay, Carolyn Holliday, Joann Johnson, Lu Klipple, Leslie Kotecki, Pam Linne, Jessica Miller, Deborah Peck and Jen "Colorful" Waddell.

The Building Bridges Facebook Discussion Group team, who for two months patiently read fragmented and run on sentences, then/than atrocities, and dared to share, care, discuss, shape and build a much stronger *Building Bridges* book. Your work is an investment not just into this book, but the Kingdom of God. The same group who may or may not have brainstormed a clever bridge building idea to reach the non-Christian 80's music loving folks with making mix tapes for their boom boxes. (Do you see what reading my words does to people!?). Thank you for making sure I didn't go "bone crazy" (well, it didn't make the content but did make the Acknowledgements page!): Mary Bankert, Natalie "Craftgirl" Booher, Jacy Christensen, Laura Gay, Christy "Silver Lining" Lee, Pam Linne, Tara Mazzawy, Mike "Token Male" Mlynarczyk, Jill Moser, Jodi "Blingalicious" Navin, Chia Richardson, Kari Pace, and Laura Stancliff.

Dr. Ivonne Ellison for her wisdom, biblical insight, friendship, prayer and patience for the past two decades.

Natalie Booher, Laura Gay, and Laura Stancliff for tirelessly editing anything and everything, like bosses, yo!

Last and certainly not least, I thank our precious Encouraged in Heart community where your love and friendship continues to embrace and encourage me to keep building, encouraging, and imperfectly living for Christ!

PREFACE

Dear Bridge Builder,

*J*esus built an eternal bridge to me. If you're a Christian, Jesus built one to you, too. Jesus' death on the cross is a sacred bridge from death to eternal life.

I wrote *Building Bridges* because I saw gaps; gaps which needed bridges. There's a world out there that doesn't know Jesus loves them or worse yet, have been so injured and marginalized by Christians they've dismissed Christ altogether. Every Christian's job is not just to get to heaven; it's to share the gospel and create more disciples (Matthew 28:16-20). Some Christians are building bridges, some don't know how to, while other Christians have fallen asleep on the job. I wrote the book to encourage all Christians to keep building, start building or wake up and get building inside and outside our churches for God's glory.

The research for this book comes from my life. When we share our life story, we bridge hearts together. You'll read that I'm incredibly flawed and still not a magnificent bridge builder, but time and time again, I've experienced God do BIG things with my imperfect efforts. I'll never be able to offer God my perfection, but I can and have offered Him my heart. I share from my life because I believe the world needs more "real", authentic and imperfect people to show off their weaknesses as a demonstration of God's beautiful strength. I share seven stories and bridge-building concepts, which I pray encourage you to boldly build:

1. God is alive and wants to use you.
2. Judging is God's job; loving is our job.
3. People are hurting and need their pain acknowledged, not overlooked.
4. Life-changing ministry occurs both inside and outside church building walls.
5. Forgiveness changes hearts.
6. We all have gaps, every last one of us.

7. God made you on purpose for a purpose to go and make more disciples.

I included questions at the end of each chapter for personal reflection and/or group discovery. I hope you read and discuss this book with a friend, a group of friends or ministry team. I pray you're encouraged to build bridges to more hearts for God's glory!

Imperfectly Building,
Steph

Chapter 1

KEEP CALM AND
BUILD BRIDGES

Where you go, I'll go
Where you stay, I'll stay
When you move, I'll move
I will follow you
Lyrics from I Will Follow by Chris Tomlin

*I*t was a hot summer afternoon and I had just finished my shift as a short order cook/waitress. I worked this same job throughout high school and during college breaks when I was home. I needed to complete one last summer course before I'd be a college graduate, which was just days away. I was ready to leave New Jersey to start my new job and life in Georgia.

Leaving work, I had the strangest thought to go to the local bookstore, a bookstore I had never visited in my twenty-one years of living in the same small town. I had no idea what was going on. This was one of the strangest and strongest inner-urgings I had ever experienced. I felt pressed to get to the bookstore — magnetized even.

After parking my used gold Chrysler Sebring convertible in front, I wandered toward the bookstore and began to question why I was there. I wrestled with this same question many times before in my two short years as a Christian: *Why was I here? What was my purpose?* This day I added another question to the mix: *Why was I following this gut feeling?* I never experienced anything like this before.

Still focused on my questions, I walked to the "Religion" section and sifted through books. I examined the contents of one when a voice behind me asked if there was another copy of the book I held.

As I turned, a message flooded my heart with a powerful intensity and stuck on auto repeat. "Tell her I love her and haven't left her. Tell her I love her and haven't left her. Tell her I love her and haven't left her."

I started to sweat as I contemplated my own level of sanity. *Is this why I'm here, to speak these words to this woman?* Surely it wasn't. God knew I hadn't figured this whole "Christian living" thing out.

"Tell her I love her and haven't left her. Tell her I love her and haven't left her. Tell her I love her and haven't left her."

I bought some time and replied, "I don't know, let's go check it out." I led the woman to a more secluded section of the bookstore.

This sentence and urgency continued. "Tell her I love her and haven't left her. Tell her I love her and haven't left her. Tell her I love her and haven't left her."

During the few seconds we walked, I wondered if God was speaking to me. I wondered if I was crazy. I wondered if I was crazy to think God would speak to me. I'd never had anything like this happen to me before.

I decided I'd tell her not because I was brave, but because I was a chicken. I figured I'd never see her again since I was soon moving to Georgia. By the time she figured out that I was out of my mind, I'd be in Georgia and never have to face the shame of another person knowing I was a lunatic. This would be Georgia's issue to face.

I looked her in the eyes, "Listen, I'm not crazy. I'm just someone who loves Jesus. I've never had this happen to me before. I believe God wants me to tell you that He loves you and hasn't left you."

She immediately collapsed into my arms, sobbed and confided that she wrestled with ending her own life.

WHOA.

I tightly hugged her, relieved I risked. I was crazy then; crazy about Jesus but not yet confident He could use me because I had a less than stellar past. But Jesus doesn't focus on our pasts, He sees our potential.

Not only did He see my potential, He created the opportunity for me to use the words and skills He put into me, to help two women; one who was about to end her life and the other who didn't see her potential.

We stayed in the bookstore and talked for a while. When we parted, she held a Bible in her hand and hope in her heart. I was humbled and changed.

I didn't consider myself one of God's varsity players, yet He allowed me to have a part of His big game plan that day in the small town bookstore. My new friend left comforted and I left in awe. All authentic God encounters should contain these two basic dimensions: holy awe (even terror) together with, and at the same time as, divine comfort and grace.[1]

In the bookstore and countless other times, I felt scared to go public about my love for Jesus. I didn't want to become one of those weird fanatics like the ones in college who asked me if I was "born again". I hadn't the foggiest clue what they were talking about and if they smoked some funny stuff right before they asked me.

I gave defensive responses back like, "I was born once, I don't need to be born again" because the question made me confused, angry and defensive, like they were in some cool club, but they wouldn't show me their special handshake to let me in their club.

Thinking back, if they used different language instead of "born again", (which I do consider myself now that I've learned the lingo – I repented, and accepted a personal relationship with Jesus Christ and have been spiritually reborn; I am a born-again Christian!) and took the time to invest in me past their fancy-foreign language, I might have considered Jesus. Their foreign language frustrated and pushed me further from wanting to pursue Jesus.

God could have certainly used someone more faithful, braver and smarter back in the bookstore, not someone who went to church and tried to change but still partied and got drunk on the weekends.

God saw my potential outside of my current life choices. God's potential is always bigger than our choices. I just hadn't figured out how to live out my love for Jesus. To be honest with you, I still haven't figured it all out. I'm still learning. Some days when I feel exasperated about this, I tell myself, "If I had everything all figured out, what would I need Jesus for?"

One of things I'm learning how to do to better is to use less "Christianese" words with non-Christians. Far too many times I've used now familiar-to-me-Christian terms and I've pushed people away from the One I love, Jesus. I forgot about how it made me feel like an outsider.

To someone who is not a Christian, using Christianese language like "born again" or "saved" to identify someone as a Christian is like speaking fluent Spanish when they've not signed up for Spanish class. They don't have the foggiest idea what you're talking about and just think you're showing off and possibly smoking some funny stuff, too.

When building bridges, if I speak the same language but need a translator, then I'm not an effective bridge builder. The bible says people who love Jesus are His ambassadors (2 Corinthians 5:20). Ambassadors strategically use terms which are familiar to the people they're sent to serve and connect with. Effective ambassadors consider the people they serve first and their own comfort level, second. It's our job as Christ's ambassadors to extend past our comfort levels and familiar language to show others just how much they're loved!

The words we speak are vital in building bridges. Often when Christians are trying to communicate their heart and faith to non-Christians, there's a language barrier. I asked my Encouraged in Heart Facebook page friends for help identifying some popular (and often confusing) words Christians use which could delay bridge building. The following is a list I made from their responses:

~ Altar call (When non-Christians are offered to come forward, often during a church service, and begin a personal relationship with Christ.)

~ Backsliding (Moving away from God.)

~ Testimony (Your personal God story.)

~ Witness (Agreeing with a Christian about a God involved encounter.)

~ Traveling mercies (Safety when traveling.)

~ Believer (Christian.)

~ Seeker (Non-Christian interested in Christianity.)

~ Private time (Time spent alone praying to God or reading the Bible.)

~ Flesh (When acting in an impulsive and non-God-centered way.)
~ The Word (The Bible.)
~ The lost (Non-Christians.)

The Gospel message isn't complicated and can be communicated in simple terms to facilitate better understanding. Jesus used few words in His time on earth as a human form. His messages were powerful. We don't need to use big words to reach people. In fact, the opposite is true. We will reach more people when we communicate the message simply and succinctly!

The words we speak are crucial. The few words I spoke in the bookstore were from God: simple, clear and concise. Humans complicate the Gospel. I believe the most dangerous member of the Christian church is the mouth. Our words are powerful. We can build others up when we speak life-giving words or we can tear others down when we speak critical and judgmental words. Our words matter and will build or burn bridges. Before you speak words, remember to "keep calm and build a bridge." Consider the words you are about to speak and ask, "Will this build or burn a bridge?" (Proverbs 25:15) Our purpose is to build by speaking life and God's truths.

Understanding my purpose also wasn't as complicated as I made it out to be. God revealed why I am here on this earth. It's not to be perfect: it's to imperfectly live for Him, encourage hearts and to build bridges. Actually, building bridges is our corporate purpose as Christians.

If we keep calm, despite feeling crazy or uncomfortable, God will use us to build bridges to hurting hearts for God's glory. This is what Jesus did for me. He built a cross shaped bridge to my hurting heart and called me friend. The cross represents a sacred bridge from death to eternal life in Heaven. Jesus brought me be back to life and the very least I can do is build bridges in gratitude.

There will be times God will ask you to build bridges with friends and other times God will ask you to build alone; like that day I was in the bookstore. Sometimes building feels a little lonely. Whenever you feel alone, remember this equation: **God + me = WE and WE > me.** You're never building alone. God is with you and will guide you. When you keep calm and build bridges, remember there's power in WE, which is able to do great things in and through you to reach a lost and hurting world.

When you are afraid to share your faith or be used by God in a new/different way, remember, "*Keep calm and build a bridge*". It's not build a bridge and get over it; it's build a bridge and get to it — the precious hearts that need to know God loves them and hasn't left them. Keep calm, build a bridge and tell them.

Discussion Questions:

1. Journal/share your thoughts on this chapter.
2. How did the bookstore story make you feel?
3. Do you believe God speaks to people today? Why or why not?
4. Have you ever felt like you lived a dual life? When?
5. Have you ever felt nervous to share your faith? When? How did you deal with it?
6. What bridges has God asked you to build? Describe the details.
7. Do you think Christians are doing a good job at building bridges in the world today?
8. Where have you seen (in your life or news media) Christians successfully and unsuccessfully build bridges?
9. If you're a Christian, do you understand you are God's ambassador?
10. Do you use any Christianese words? Which ones? Do you need to change this to be best heard?
11. How have you successfully built bridges?

Chapter 2

IF I ONLY KNEW THEN
WHAT I KNOW NOW

*There is nothing noble about being superior
to your fellow man; the true nobility is being
superior to your former self.*
Ernest Hemingway

I sat in Mrs. Shuba's honor's English class my high school sophomore year and seethed with hate. *Tina sat a few rows away and smiled, which only made me stew more.

How dare she smile. I know what she did. How does she live with herself?

Tina and I had a mutual friend, *Rita. Rita drove Tina to her abortion a few days earlier, despite my lengthy pleas.

I didn't like Tina nor was I close friends with her, but Rita and I were close. Rita and Tina were close. I couldn't stand to see Tina smile after I knew what she had done. I was raised in a very pro-life Catholic Church and family. Tina's smile made me angry because I wanted to see her look miserable. So I took matters into my own miserable hands.

I passed Tina a note in class, "I know what you did and I think you're disgusting."

Interestingly, the author of this note was voted "Most Friendly" by the senior class. What a fraud, huh? There was nothing friendly or productive about my miserable hate note.

Tina never responded back.

I can't truly capture how ashamed I am to share this story with you. If only I knew then what

I know now. I thought the way I handled Tina *was* godly. If I only knew then what I know now, I would have realized I wasn't behaving godly, I was being a judgmental and condemning jerk.

Did you know that in 2013, "Judge Judy" Sheindline was paid $47 million dollars in 2013 for judging people?[1] Funny thing is, I judge for free. And as I've judged, I've limited my God-ordained bridge building opportunities. I can't love a person as God desires while judging him or her.

If only I knew then that Jesus doesn't want us to judge others. Judgment will happen and it falls under God's job description, not mine (Ecclesiastes 12:14). I can judge circumstances and situations, but not people. For example, I need to exercise wise judgment in whether I'll enter a situation, circumstance or relationship, but this is entirely different than judging another person.

Popular American evangelical Christian pastor and author Rick Warren tweeted, "Stop judging how far people still have to go. Start celebrating how far they've come."[2]

When I lost needed weight, I didn't want people to keep reminding me how much more weight I needed to lose. Believe me, I knew. All I wanted was to be celebrated for how far I'd come. The world needs to hear more positive and less "not good enough" messages.

I've made some progress. I still find my inner Judge Judy pop up. Many years and friendships later, I've judged less and cared more. The shift occurred when I stopped talking about how wrong I think abortion (or whatever the "thing" I've judged) is and invested love into the person: listening, bridging, connecting and caring.

In listening, I often learned the guilt and shame of people's past still remains many years later. I also found their healing was often delayed because many mislead-well-intentioned-judgmental Christians judged instead of loved.

What if non-Christians knew more about what Christians are for, like loving God and loving others, than what we are against? Judging others is like another type of hate note being sent straight to their heart, which says, "I know what you did and I think you're disgusting. Not good enough." Friends of Jesus don't condemn you for your past or make you feel less than them. Friends of Jesus remind you, "Repent. You're forgiven (if you ask for it) and are loved (Luke 5:20)."

What exacerbates this for me is how often I see people, who have had abortions, be condemned, but somehow "holy" me, who wrote a hate note and murdered a person with my words and who also had premarital sex but never got pregnant, was cleared? I see other versions of sexual impurity within the church like pornography, lust of stuff and others, out of marriage sex (physically and emotionally), etc. that get swept under the carpet while others get pulled onto the carpet.

I think we need to pull all fellow sinners in closer; not push them farther away from us and Jesus. Speaking specifically to post-abortion friends, I've observed a whole new wave of grief, pain and shame resurface when they've held a newborn baby and remember their never held baby.

I'm a mother now. Becoming a mother changes you. Know what? Not becoming a mother changes you, too. I had three miscarriages before I birthed our son, Jake. I'm telling you that not becoming a mother changes you. I may not know what it's like having an abortion but I do know what it's like not holding a baby in your arms. I know that not becoming a mother when you were once pregnant, it changes you.

Not all women and men need, or want, to talk about their past lives, but some may. The subject of abortion is just one of the many subjects which I've observed as judged in the Christian community. I believe Christians need to be agents of healing by letting others share their stories, lives and pasts: talking and sharing your life story is a huge part of becoming friends and beginning the healing process. This starts with asking God for forgiveness after you've confessed your errors. All of our sins are forgiven through Christ no matter how big or small. Sin is sin; sin separates (Isaiah 59:2). We need to show compassion and be conduits of Jesus's forgiveness instead of reservoirs of judgment.

Remember, you don't have to agree with people to let them share their scars and stories. You just need to listen; and if they want to hear about your story and scars, boldly share yours.

One of the many things I love about authentic Jesus-lovers is that they have scars, and they're not afraid to use them as bridges to hearts. They follow Jesus's story-sharing example and when the Holy Spirit prompts, they share the stories behind their scars. As a result, lives are changed.

Scars are opportunities to share about the reality of Jesus in your life.

Bridges are built when we listen, care and share.

I remember sitting in a Christian women's conference where the speaker shared that about forty percent of the women in any audience have had an abortion. I couldn't get the number out of my head. Roughly one-third of women will have an abortion during their reproductive lifetimes.[3]

Believe me: when I write, I see the hypocrisy in myself. I see hypocrisy within the church walls, too. None of us are perfect and, in our imperfections, we hurt others. I want to judge and hurt others a lot less. I need Jesus's grace, love and forgiveness and want to be a conduit of such unmerited awesomeness.

I no longer wonder why many don't want to come into the church community or building and explore a relationship with Jesus. It hurts to be around some Jesus people when you're defined by what you've done (your past) instead of who you are becoming (your future).

Do you know what else I see, besides thick hypocrisy (in myself and fellow Christians)? I see hurting people: hurting people that don't want to come into the church building because of my and others hurtful hypocrisy.

When people don't feel safe to come just as they are, they just won't come...into our homes, hearts and churches. They will go, however, to wherever their pain can be numbed, which can morph into addictive behaviors; like work, drugs, alcohol, food, sex and even over-serving, all to avoid pain.

As I wrote this chapter, I had major shame for being such a mean girl to Tina. My shame of my past sin became writer's block: shame blocks healthy love and life-flow.

I've learned some more things along my life journey and know the antidote to shame. It's not more condemnation. It's forgiveness. I needed to ask for forgiveness. I prayed and asked Jesus to please forgive me for writing such a horrible hate note. I then found Tina on social media and wrote her an entirely different note this time. I apologized for the horrible note I sent her in high school and asked her to forgive me. Unlike that day in Mrs. Shuba's class, Tina wrote back. Her message was one of kindness, grace and forgiveness.

My friends, being forgiven feel so incredibly good. So good I want to replicate this to others.

As I read her kind words, I felt unworthy of such kindness and grace. This is similar to how Jesus makes me feel. Loved. Accepted. Forgiven.

I can't change what I wrote to Tina back then, but I can let my past change me for the better. I can ask God and those I've injured for forgiveness. Sometimes all we need is to be reminded of the fact that we are forgiven. Forgiveness comes in the form of God's grace. Grace is a big concept to capture. Jesus's grace is bigger than anything we could ever capture. Jesus' grace is released when we wholeheartedly ask Him and others for forgiveness. Like what Tina gifted me in her response.

I wonder what would happen if Christians judged less and loved more. Particularly so, when it's uncomfortable and when we need to dig a little deeper within ourselves in areas where we disagree, to recognize the bigger job at hand: to share the hope, love, forgiveness and grace Jesus has to offer.

I'm not the same person I was yesterday. God's helped me make some needed changes. I judge less and love others more but I still have a long way to go.

I've seen the damage some well-intentioned Christians, like myself, have done. Part of my job is writing and another part is speaking. The very first women's retreat I spoke at years ago had over 100 women attend. As I opened the second session, I sensed the Holy Spirit prompt me to share about abortion and encourage women who had an abortion to know God loves them, to ask Him for forgiveness and to know they're forgiven. Period.

This was not in my notes.

*Julie came up after and thanked me because she had an abortion, healed and now helps women work through their grief and shame and uses her life story to point other's to Jesus. Unlike Tina, who I pushed away with my cruel words, I pulled Julie in and hugged her tight.

What if we all hugged more than condemned?

While some may not agree with my views, perspective or stance, we can talk about our differences and both learn from each other. More importantly, care about each other.

Matthew 7:3 asks a profound question, *Why do you look at the speck of sawdust in your brother's eye and pay no attention to the plank in your own eye?*

If I only knew then that those planks in my own eyes, they blocked me from seeing what God had planned ahead of me. I used my self-righteousness plank to bat at Tina when in reality God wanted me to drop my plank to cross over and lift Tina up, minimally, in prayer. You see it wasn't until I dropped the self-righteous and judgmental planks (twenty years later) to cross over and see that Tina was God's child.

When we take the planks out and lay them down, it's only then we can cross over into purpose, to reach out and get to the splinter folks.

This is what the Apostle Paul did. God took the self-righteous religious planks out of his eyes, which gave Paul a new purpose and vision. Even prison bars didn't limit his bridge building. He still had a working mouth behind bars, so he continued to worship and praise God. As a result, doors opened and chains dropped (Acts 16:26). Paul still had hands, so he wrote letters to build bridges. Nothing, no one, no circumstances stopped him from dropping planks down to build bridges out! Listen, when God wakes and walks you into purpose, you'll start doing things like getting up early or staying up later or going to different places to get to the hearts that need to know Jesus loves them! You'll see prison bars as a perfectly suitable opportunity to build bridges.

The beauty here is that the very same planks, which blinded Paul, became the vital bridge building material God asked Paul to lay down where he crossed over to the "sawdust" people!

When I focus on the little things, the sawdust in others I can easily minimize and forget about my own BIG plank stuff. When I recognize the plank in my *own eye*, God helps me lay those same planks down to cross over to an entirely new purpose and mission!

It's time to drop those planks down and come up higher. It's bridge building time! Let go of fake holy to rise UP and live out God's purpose. I hate to write this, but some of the many planks I've dropped, I've picked back up. Be patient with the work God is doing in your life and in other's lives.

Patience is one of the words used to describe God's love in 1 Corinthians 13 and also one way we see fruit of the Holy Spirit (Galatians 5:22) come true in our life.

What if when we see young women and men who had babies out of wedlock, instead of condemning and judging them, we pull them and their babies closer to our hearts and consider they did have other options, like abortion? What would happen if we helped them and their babies live and fulfill their dreams and not allow their lives to be defined by one moment? What if we remembered we all have sin in our past and want to be accepted before we feel safe to change anything? What if we all loved instead of judged others for their shortcomings, sins and failures? What would it look like if people could come into a church and really focus on their relationship with God and grow instead of experiencing isolating judgment?

We have all done things we want to change or that we regret. We will probably continue to do or say things we wish we hadn't after the fact. I go to church to grow closer not further to God and to thank Him for His never ending grace. The reality is that some won't come to church because all they experience in church is more judgmental pain.

I love how Jesus stood up for the adulteress and told those who held judgment stones ready to stone her to death, *"Let any one of you who is without sin be the first to throw a stone at her."*[4] Beloved evangelist Billy Graham said, "It is the Holy Spirit's job to convict, God's job to judge and my job to love."

God made me with two eyes, two ears, two nostrils, two hands and two feet but only one mouth. I need to watch, listen, smell, hold, hug, help and walk much more than I talk. Our words have power and we need to use them to encourage and build others up (1 Thessalonians 5:11), not tear them down.

The words that come out of our mouths tell a hurting world what we think about them and our Jesus. Our words have power. Our words can serve as a powerful bridge to build people up or tear them down. I've asked God to help me build bridges to share His hope with hurting, isolated hearts. Sometimes it's with hugs, sometimes it's by listening and sometimes it's with words.

If only I knew then what I know now. I wouldn't have sent the horrible note to Tina. I would have dared to be an all-together different type of messenger; a bridge building messenger of God's hope and love.

*Names changed to protect privacy.

Discussion Questions:

1. Journal/share your thoughts on this chapter.
2. How did you feel reading about Steph's note to Tina? Have you ever written or spoken a judgmental note like this?
3. Have you ever thought, "If only I knew then, what I know now?" When? Is there a bridge building opportunity found?
4. Has there ever been a time church has felt unsafe to you? When? Why was it unsafe?
5. Do you see hypocrisy in Christian churches? Where?
6. Have you've ever felt like a hypocrite? When? How did you change?
7. How do you think Christians should handle differences and sin to invite more people in?
8. When has someone apologized to you, which made a difference in your life?
9. What does Matthew 7:3-5 mean to you?

Chapter 3

LEAD WITH LOVE

The people you have at your table tells a lot about the Jesus you follow. Deb Hirsch

*I*t was an exceptionally dark time in my life. My father had just died. Days after I buried my father, I learned my husband had cancer (he was treated and healed!). A week later, my husband, who had breathed for me as I grieved Dad's death, was on an overseas work trip. To add to the mix, our kids had their third consecutive week of snow days. I wondered when I'd stop grieving and chronically rescheduling life. I questioned whether I would be able to focus, at least for a few moments, on work, because I needed a distraction to the grief process. I felt overwhelmed, exhausted, fuzzy and numb. Just doing regular daily life was like trying to push play dough through a drinking straw; difficult and only possible with a lot of forceful work.

Then the gift arrived. A rare sunny Sunday in the middle of winter, which mimicked an early spring day. The following day's forecast predicted yet more snow, which in northern Virginia meant more snow days, and inevitable more rescheduling. In a moment of rare clarity, I decided to take my kids out to get some exercise, vitamin D, and "pushed the play dough through" to the local tennis court.

We brought our four-legged child, Crash, with us. I figured he'd appreciate a different view other than the view from our brown recliner. For days, Crash sat attached to my hip in a faithful silent vigil as his chronically tearful mother mourned.

I latched Crash to the nearby bleacher and the boys and I got our tennis on. It proved to be the most fun I had in what felt like forever. The sunrays and laughter cracked through the thick monotonous layer of grief.

As we prepared to head home to get showered for church, the boys put our gear in the car while I walked Crash for a final pee. I noticed our friend, *John, walked toward me while Crash searched for the perfect grass blade. My family and I had known and loved John and his family for the past ten years. I hadn't seen John since my father passed.

The first thing John said to me wasn't, "Hi!" or, "How have you been doing, Steph?" No, John came over to stoically reprimand me because I broke the local rule by having my dog on the community property. A rule I had no idea about. I tried to shake off being offended, but I couldn't. I was in a funk. The truth is, I didn't know about the rule. And, after I learned about the rule, I still didn't care. I could barely get my teeth brushed let alone care about some rule. My entire goal for the day was to just make it through.

I arrived to the tennis court that day grief-stricken. I left exponentially worse after being reprimanded by John, a person I still love and call friend. Now that I see clearly, my friend wasn't trying to attack me. I was just in a bad place. I know this because I know John and me. Our families had walked a lot of life miles together. He's normally a very gregarious and kind guy, but this day he was stoic and serious because I broke a rule; a rule, which I felt that day, was more important to him than his friend Steph. Ouch.

I tried to make a quick joke and get out of there. I didn't feel like talking about my feelings; I didn't feel safe. I just felt like hibernating. Even my joke turned south. John reminded me of his community position and why that rule was important (to him). He then went on to further explain where the rule was posted and waited so I could turn around to seek said sign out in the distance.

I'm rarely short on words. This was one of the rare days where I was short on words.

Honestly, I was so hurt my friend never even mentioned anything about my father, or asked about how I was doing. We'd been the kind of friends that have been there for each other to include our being there for him when his own father died not too long ago.

But that didn't happen that day, nothing but rules from him on a day I really could have used a friend. What hurt me even more deeply is when I shared I didn't know the rule, John went to great lengths to explain I did. I felt condescended, insulted, hurt and uncared for.

I knew about the no parking in the fire lane rule. Perhaps I take more notice to "fire-related" rules because my husband's been a firefighter for the past two decades. My eyes are more trained to notice anything related to firefighters.

I know why this rule was important to my friend. I get it. And I didn't respect it. I understand why John would wisely say something to his good friend, Steph. Seriously, I get it. On a different day, I might have been much more willing to listen, but on this day, I didn't even remotely care. I was absorbed in my grief season and only wanted to push the play dough through to the end of the straw (day).

I drove home in tears because I was in a very raw and vulnerable state. My friend's insensitivity intensified the pain I carried to the tennis court. Honestly, I felt like John was so laser focused on the rule, he forgot about his friend. I felt like he chose to let his community position take priority over the person in front of him, his friend, Steph. If I didn't already know and love John, one encounter would have made me avoid him like the plague in the future.

Now before I make John sound like a total jerk, he's not. He's a really great guy and remains a great friend to this day. I want you to remember, I was in a really bad place. I know John well and this is not John's normal pattern of behavior, nor mine. He is a good guy. Honest.

I use this story not to put my friend on the roaster, but as a first-hand story about how we as Christians often lead with the rules of Christianity as opposed to the love of Christ. Sometimes we can let our position be prioritized over people who are hurting. What we're forgetting about is there are hurting hearts that do not care about our Bible rules because they don't see us first care about them.

If you remember nothing else from this book, remember this statement: lead with the love of Christ, not the laws of Christianity.

Simply put, lead with love, not the law.

When we Christians look down our long noses at other people's sins such as premarital sex or drug abuse and we tell them "our rules" (forgetting that we might have experimented with sin in our past and present); we should look down our own long noses at ourselves first. Remember what pain feels like. We can bridge to more hearts when we lead with caring love and after they feel safe and loved, share about the rules which are important in our lives.

I was recently thinking about why I sin. I expanded it wider to WHY people sin. Why do you think we sin?

Is it to mask or escape pain? Is it for a "fun"? Are we "looking for love in all the wrong places?"

The empty need we are trying to fill is the first priority. Love is the first priority. Pure love. God's love. God is love. We humans often seek out "love" or fraudulent representations of love, to get our love need met. Often those who are the most difficult to love, are the ones who need love the most. Remember this and help me remember this cause loving others can be really, really difficult.

If we don't love, then we don't love God because God is love (1John 4:8). I love the Word of God. It's changed my life and given me freedom I've never known. Yes, the rules in the Bible have given me freedom.

Who are we to tell others about our rules before we first dare to care, or at least pretend to care, remembering we all are strugglers in need of love?

Remember how horrifically I handled Tina in chapter 2? I didn't dare to care for her. It would have been better and more godly to have written nothing at all than to write an angry hate note. Sure, there's a time for correction and to speak truth in love (Ephesians 4:15). Only fools don't get help and correction (Proverbs 15:32). But it's *how* we love and correct as well as welcome others into our hearts and homes that will build or burn bridges.

When you go visit someone at his or her home, which scenario do you prefer?

Scenario 1: Ding-dong. The door opens to a stoic face and a, "Take your shoes off."

I know when this happens I am left with an initial, "Ummmm, okay." and wonder if I'm interrupting this person's day.

OR

Scenario 2: Ding-dong. The door opens to a warm smile and a, "Come on in! I'm so happy you're here!"

Which of the two scenarios sound more welcoming to you?

I choose scenario two.

After you warmly welcome and invite someone into your home and heart, then you can share both your rules and preferences like where to put your shoes or jacket.

When someone comes to the Fink home, it's important to me our guests feel at home. I want visitors to feel loved because my cooking is bad and I want to be hospitable.

I want to lead with love, not the law (or our house-human-made-rules).

And since you're (not) asking, I do have a preference. Our house rule is for people to take their shoes off. It's not a deal-breaker, but it is my preference. But really, what's the worst that could happen if people didn't take their shoes off? Maybe I'd have to scrub some dirt off the floor later? Well, their spot could be added to the many others, which still need some attention even as I write this.

Sometimes Christians allow their positions, preferences, comforts and their realities to build tall walls, which prevent bridges from being built. I use this small example because I've seen so many people "put off" and wounded by Christians who declared their love of rules more passionately than their love of God or others. Wounded like I was by John that day. The difference is that I know John. I have a history with him and know we're both not normally like this. It's unfortunate we both had an off day.

But what about the people you don't have a history built with? Too many non-Christians don't have a positive history of friendship to fall back on in relation to the Christian community. I often observe many Christians in mainstream media be highlighted to look like insensitive, narrow-minded, love my rules then I'll love you kind of people. We may only get ONE chance to build a bridge. Let's make it count. Let's build, not burn, a bridge down.

Some of you may be thinking, "Well Steph, you're just being ridiculous. When I come to your place, just tell me to take my shoes off, it's no big deal." I get what you're saying. Honestly. I'm going to tell you something I tell my hubby and kiddos while often high atop my own soapbox. It's not what you say, it's how you say it. It's okay to speak your preferences, rules, etc, but it's really in *how* you say it. And when and I speak my statement from my soapbox, I'm normally yelling so really I'm not the best messenger of the statement.

If I intentionally communicate in a caring and respectful way, I'll probably (not always) be heard. If I am communicating in a caring and respectful way, I'll probably (not always, cause I'm thick-headed) listen.

When John approached me, I knew historically he loved and cared for me. He could have made a world of difference if he asked about me first, especially in my grief season, BEFORE he shared the rule. It would have made a difference. It says in Psalm 34:18 that, "The Lord is close to the brokenhearted" and I believe Christians need to be also.

Our marriage counselor, Mary Baker, shared this wisdom with my husband and I one day in session, "Start with empathy, then communicate your boundary."

When we begin with caring empathy, hardened hearts often soften. It is so very important to have boundaries. When boundaries are spoken in the right time, God's time, bridges are built from painful isolation to loving connection. You can trust God's timing even when you don't understand exactly what's going on, like I didn't in the bookstore that day.

Remember, "Keep calm and build a bridge."

Foundations have to be poured before bridges are constructed. Love is the foundation we Christians need to pour to build solid, lasting bridges where two-way communications become possible.

Use wisdom in how you communicate and intentionally build those love bridges to hurting hearts. God provides many doors of opportunity and how we treat the stranger or friend at the front door of our homes and our hearts matters.

There are too many times I've allowed my preferences to prohibit my compassion and hospitality. Like, when I've waited for a repairperson for eight hours and they show up after the eighth hour. Heck, even when the repair person shows up in the first hour, many times my nose is out of whack because I needed to block out so much of my day for them to come and you know, do their job.

My preference is that people don't swear around me. I've made some progress, but still have some slips. My preference is for people to never say, "OMG" because it really hurts my heart. I love God so much and my heart hurts when I hear God or Jesus' names used in disparaging ways. I sometimes share my preference because it hurts my heart, but it is usually after I know someone and we've built some type of relationship. My rule is that I don't use God's name in a jacked up way. My preference is for others to do the same, but if they don't subscribe to my rulebook, the Bible, then I need to grow up and realize my rule isn't important to them. Yet. I can pray for opportunities to share why my rule is important to me normally after we have the love foundation poured and set.

Think about it, if you just met someone and they kept correcting and interrupting you, how would you feel about it? I know me. I'd make sure to take the long way around next time. I'd either avoid or instigate them. Just saying.

Christians need to confidently share their beliefs with others, but when you bombard too quickly, it scares people away and makes them avoid you. It's so important to find that happy balance and introduce them to Jesus in a way that makes them feel safe and not like they are being lectured to the point that they totally shut down. Each relationship is different.

Sometimes (not always), I have to let go of my little preferences to see the big God picture. When people feel safe to come as they are, they will come and share and two people will grow and change.

God puts different people in our lives to help us not be the same and to mature us as human beings and Christians.

When people don't feel safe to come just as they are, they just won't come...into our homes, hearts and churches. South African-born missiologist, author, and a leader in the missional church movement, Alan Hirsch, says that 60% of Americans say they would never go to any church.[1]

This statistic is staggering and evidence Christians need to echo Christ's love. I'm not saying compromise your values or faith, I'm saying be patient. Remember, love is patient, kind, hopeful and perseverant; not proud, boastful or easily angered (1 Corinthians 13:4-7).

If you're a math person, maybe this will fit your computations: love multiplies, hate divides.

When people feel accepted and loved, look out, its game on! Consider for a moment when people are initiated or "jumped" into gangs. People will kill other people and endure heinous things just to be accepted into a community.

I feel like we need to go the distance, allow some stones to be thrown at us and continue building bridges. Lives are at stake.

When I know someone genuinely cares for me, I'm eager to learn more about them, which includes their preferences, personal rules and laws. This is all part of building bridges to hurting hearts.

God is love (1 John 4:8). Love builds bridges. Love is a patient bridge builder. Bridges take time to build and they are built over a period of time and stand steady in a foundation of love. Bridges are burned when people feel judged, criticized or looked down on.

Be patient when building bridges. Consider your building approach and methods. Dare to care, share and nurture the hearts you've dared to reach. Then watch them return the favor. Then they become invested in things and even preferences that are important to you.

I have a lot of preferences. One of the things I don't prefer is to wait. I don't like waiting for anyone or anything. At my last OB/GYN appointment, I waited for an hour and I was smoking hot mad. I'd been with this practice for over a decade and never had to wait this long. My preference is not to be put in a waiting/holding pattern of any kind.

I was still able to work from the waiting room so it really wasn't that big of a deal, but my preference is still my preference. And, I have a type A personality too. So I'm a real party to hang out with. I quickly get irritated when I can't check things off my day's "To Do" list.

It wasn't until after I sat in a paper gown on the exam table and waited for my doctor that I realized I sat in a bridge building moment. I can exercise one of many options: say nothing, say something, be passive aggressive and state how long I waited. I had lots of options.

Then I remembered how I adore and trust my doctor. He delivered both Cal and Jake and had seen parts of me that well...few have. When he came into the room, I met him eye-to-eye and smiled. I could tell by his flushed pink cheeks he was in the middle of a rough day. He's normally chill, this day he seemed frazzled.

I built a bridge and said, "You must be having a rough day because you're never running this behind. One of the things I like most about you is that you take the time to invest and talk with your patients as friends. I really value that about you. I hope you know how wonderful you are."

I saw a mild drop in his shoulders and he alluded to the fact that there were some difficulties. He obviously couldn't go into details because of patient privacy protections. I built a proactive and intentional bridge and stifled my preference because love is patient and considers others. My preference of not waiting wasn't a big deal. Loving and caring for him was the bigger deal.

I can't even begin to tell you how many times I behaved so arrogantly because I was more concerned about my preferences of not wanting to, "waste my time" and assert, "my time is valuable" "my God rules are important" (and they are!) where in fact I just wasted a perfectly good opportunity to live out my God rules of LOVE my neighbor.

So many non-Christians in this world honestly don't care about the Christian rules, which they digest as preferences, elitism, and exclusivity. Jesus was inclusive. His love compelled not repelled. I pray my life contagiously compels others towards Christ.

Do you know why some people don't care about our preferences and God rules?

Because we haven't cared nearly enough about them.

Because they often feel judged more than loved.

Because they observe Christians break those rules. (The IT factor again).

Do you know what *is* desirable? To be loved like Jesus loves which is a grace-filled, relentless, forgiving, merciful, non-condemning love. I cannot replicate a perfect love. I am not that awesome. But I can sure stretch and try.

When our flaws arise, as I know mine sure do, the history of friendship and love will help cover the flaws because that's what love does. Love covers (1 Peter 4:8). My love for John covered that Sunday at the tennis court. I hope and pray that

John's love continues to be patient and covers me and my many flaws and shortcomings, like when I bring my dog to the tennis court. (Which I haven't since that day, okay? Honest.)

It's important to keep your rules and preferences, but don't make a regular practice of prioritizing anything higher than love. To do so can delay, destruct and burn down our bridge building efforts.

I want to make one last point before I close this chapter out. Christians are infamous for highlighting or prioritizing certain rules, sins and the like.

I'm going to lead with me. My friends, this is routinely a great place to start. Start with yourself instead of picking on other people. It's humbling and necessary. I am a food addict. A glutton. I've struggled in my food relationship my entire life. My first book, *28 Lessons I Learned When My Head Was Stuck in the Fridge*, is about my food addiction recovery. A recovery which still continues one meal and day at a time.

I can go into many churches and be met with large quantities of high calorie food. My sin of gluttony is celebrated and often enabled in "safe" places, churches. If I were a drug addict, I wouldn't find rows of cocaine, or marijuana joints, waiting in the lobby for me to snort and smoke because it's not socially acceptable in the church culture. But a hearty casserole and cake-filled pot-luck though...

I've observed a growing trend to highlight certain non-socially acceptable behaviors higher than my sins. Listen. Without Jesus, we are all in a sinking ship. No one's better. We're all fellow strugglers and striders. Make sure you remember this. Just because I'm a food addict doesn't make my sin less serious.

What I'm about to write next might sound crazy to you, but here it goes. I can't tell you how many times I've thanked God for my food addiction because it continues to humble me down to nothing but who I am; a desperate, struggling Jesus lover who needs Him every moment and meal of every day. (2 Corinthians 12:7-10)

I forgot how desperate I was after I learned some Bible verses. I got puffy proud. It wasn't pretty. God doesn't like puffy proud people. He likes the humble peeps. (James 4:6)

We all struggle with something. No human being is without struggles including the person in the mirror, the person with the smallest/biggest smile, bank account and ministry. We desperately need each other. We can find comfort and commonality in our struggles and strides. Then together we can find God who faithfully meets us along the way.

Jesus is both holy and humble. Building bridges enables us to experience community and communion with Christ and others. As we humble ourselves, serve others, share struggles, preferences and stuff we're building community. Allow the people on the other side of the bridge to do likewise. Don't get puffy and think you're "better than" others.

I often need to remind myself that I don't have the power to change people; I only have the power to love them and build bridges. Each person is in charge of his or her own choices and Jesus is in charge of the changing, so we better get to loving. Obedience is my job; outcome is God's job.

One summer, my then nine year old son, Caleb, had a vision to start a sunflower seed business. He bought the seeds with his own money, carefully considered where the most sun landed in our yard, and planted seeds. He watered the seeds every day and even made a checklist to count how many days it took for his seeds to grow into seedlings.

After all his thoughtful planning and hard work he grew one little sunflower. Do you know why my son is an incredible success? Because he planted that first seed. Obedience is our job; outcome is God's job. I don't know where you need to plant a seed today, be faithful and obedient to plant, then, trust God with the outcome.

Love is a verb, which means action. We show the world our love for God by our love for others (John 13:35). Once we take the action of bridge building and follow Jesus's command, we become alive. Then we're living out part of our purpose and destiny in God's great plan!

There's a tension, often within self, of what is real and what is ideal. What is real is Christ loves everyone. What's ideal is where people's personalities, preferences, politics and persuasions come in. Don't let what's real, get superseded by what you think is ideal. We live in a real world, filled with really hurting people who need a very real Jesus. Jesus broke tons of societies' rules and built bridges to hurting, overlooked and marginalized hearts.

Let's be like Jesus and lead with love, not the law.

When you think you're being holy and righteously declaring the rules, don't forget people may have reasons why they break the rules and laws that are important to you.

Lead with love. Get to know them and their story. When you learn more about their past, the present makes more sense. God paves opportunities to share the hope of Christ for their future.

Share your scars, your story and your Jesus too. I said share not shove down their throat. God is love and love changes hearts. I know because love (God) changed my heart and life.

*Name changed to protect privacy.

Discussion Questions:

1. Journal/share your thoughts on this chapter.
2. When has someone led with his or her preferences? How did it impact you?
3. Do you have any preferences "laws" for people coming into your home? What about your church? If yes, do they need to be revised?
4. Think about a person who invested into your life. Now that you know them, did they let go of any preference to build a bridge to you? Be specific.
5. What are your thoughts about "lead with love, not the law"? Will you use this method in the future?
6. Do you believe we are all strugglers and striders in need of a Savior? Share your thoughts.
7. What's an area where you struggle? What can you do to work on these areas?
8. How did reading "60% of people will not come into church buildings" make you feel? How do you believe God will you use to decrease the percentage?
9. Do you see hypocrisy in the Christian church? Where?
10. Do you see any hypocrisy in your own life? Where?

Chapter 4

IN AND OUT

*If we spend all our time serving saved people,
blessing blessed people and disciplining discipled
people, WHEN will we have time to connect
with the lost? Jen Hatmaker*

*I*raced through reviewing my kid's homework and put dinner on the table so I could leave my home life to be on time for a church board meeting.

As I drove past *Kim's home, I thought, "Man, I wish I had more time for Kim, but I gotta get to church for the board meeting." And then I felt IT; like a big fat hypocrITe.

My neighbor, Kim, and I were newer friends. We met at our neighborhood Super Bowl party. A natural friendship evolved. Our similar senses of humor and Irish Catholic upbringings helped us click. After the Super Bowl party, we had many laughs and chats. We enjoyed one another's company and hung out together inside and outside of the neighborhood.

This is why, as I drove further from Kim and closer to church, I felt conflicted.

I loved serving on my church board. It was a huge honor to be voted one of the twelve board of directors of a large church that had a weekly attendance of around 2,500 people. I felt like I made a difference with the things I shared and voted for/against. After I was elected, I learned I was the first woman elected in over 25 years. So I felt like not only did I make a difference, but also represented a much-needed female perspective.

The first year I was elected was a relatively easy year. I was re-elected to a second term the next year, but it was a much different type of year. We faced many adventures and challenges as our senior pastor resigned, numerous staff changes took place and we considered a new church focus/vision.

Part of the new church focus was to maintain an attractional focus while also becoming more mission minded. Just in case these seem like new words to you, "attractional" basically means activities, programs and messages that would interest people to come into a church building/community. "Mission" means going outside of the building with the focus to share the Gospel by forming Christ-centered relationships and community wherever people live their lives.

We wanted to encourage our church members to reach outside the church walls and be more mission minded while still maintaining meaningful work and relationships within the walls (being attractionally minded).

I wasn't just learning about it, I lived *IT* in my own life.

I wanted to impact people within my church building walls, but not at the expense of the people outside the church walls who needed to know Christ loves them (the 60% mentioned in Chapter 3).

As much as I genuinely liked being around Kim and saw a need, I didn't have a lot of extra time to invest in her. Like most people I know, I held many life roles: Christian, wife, mom, daughter, sister, friend, neighbor, board member, speaker, writer, abolitionist, volunteer, and coffee drinker. That last role takes up a good portion of my time!

I'm not unlike most Christians. There is a tension of sorts when we think about how we will spend our time, energy, talents and money. And because I love Jesus so much, I want to serve Him with excellence. I prayed and God directed me to not accept the nomination for a third year of service. I felt guilty about leaving my board post because of the massive changes, needed female representation and also because it was an unspoken but common practice for most board members to serve three consecutive years. The bylaws allowed three consecutive years of service and then required to take one year off. I needed to remind myself numerous times that Jesus isn't the author of guilt; the devil is.

I wrested because I am a people pleaser. I didn't want to let my church, board, and congregation down. But after I prayed for quite some time, I felt released to do as I learned in the board room to meet the 60%, like Kim, while also investing in the work that occurs inside the church walls...teaching, discipling, encouraging others to courageously go into the world with the Gospel.

My son Jake, whose is currently 12 years old and has the life goal to be an NFL athlete, made a wise analogy, "Church is like the locker room, the world is like the football game." I thought this was so awesome. We need the locker room to learn, be coached and build camaraderie to kick some butt out on the field, out in the world, where we we'll make some good plays and also get injured (persecuted).

When we go outside the church walls and "get in the game" we'll get hurt. Faith in Christ is not a spectator sport. Getting injured is part of a disciple's job description. We need to get in the game, make some great plays (introduce some people to Jesus) and get hurt (persecuted for our faith). Just for the record, I'm not a huge fan of the word persecution cause it sounds really uncomfortable and could mess with my coffee drinking schedule.

While I have hurt others and been hurt inside the church, it's safer and perhaps more comfortable in the locker room where we athletes (disciples) agree we want to kick butt, but the risk of injury is exceptionally low. We have to train, prepare then get up and go out in the game!

True disciples of Christ do not just believe in God they also live out their faith in God. They get in the game. A disciple's job is not spectator based, it's participant-based. They participate under God's promptings (like in bookstores) and leadings. They watch, do and be. Not just believe in God, but also *live* out our faith in God. There are hurting people everywhere I go and this is where I personally experience IT, feeling like a hypocrite.

Kim described herself to me as a "seeker". "Seeker" is another one of those Christianese terms (on our list in Chapter 1) for someone who's interested in growing in his or her faith. She was a quick learner and knew some of the Christianese lingo, which caught my attention.

We talked about so many things, how we struggled leaving the corporate world and becoming stay at home mothers, our past, our faith, what devotions were helping in teaching us and our kids about God and the Bible, gardening (which I cannot do) and so much more.

I still remember the tension I felt as I drove further from Kim and closer to church. One of the Holy Spirit's roles is as a "Helper." The Holy Spirit specifically put the Bible story of the Good Samaritan (Luke 10:30-37) in my brain as I drove toward church that night.

There are so many rich lessons in this story, but what resonated in me this night was that there was a neighbor in need. The first two people who passed the needy neighbor, a religious leader and a church leader, were too busy and holy to stop and help. It was the Samaritan, not the "holy and religious" people, who stopped and helped. In this story, I was the church leader that walked (drove) past my neighbor in need.

To expand this story a bit wider, Jesus loved the Samaritans and went out of His way to meet Samaritans where they were. He didn't invite them into the temple, He had beautiful, meaningful and God honoring encounters where He met them along life's road.

What's also interesting to note is the religious people in Jesus' day didn't approve of the Samaritans, yet Jesus said for us to go behave like the Samaritan in this story. The red letters (meaning Jesus' words) said in Luke 10:37, *"Go and do likewise."* This means to be kind and compassionate to your neighbors. Help your neighbor in need.

I want to highlight here the Samaritan didn't bring the needy neighbor to his church and ask them to do anything. The Samaritan used his own money, resources and skills to take care of the neighbor there. That's the stuff right there. The Samaritan went to great personal and financial lengths to care for the neighbor in need.

The biggest takeaway from this story is that people will believe our actions more than our words. If we tell people that Jesus loves them (and He really, really does!), but never have time to connect and/or care for them; then we better watch IT. Our actions don't match our words. People are watching and waiting to see if Christians really do care or if they're full of IT.

So what am I writing here? Quit doing church work and be available all day to your neighbors? No. It's not church work OR neighbor hang time; it's AND. It's intentional church work and being available for neighbor hang time. We need both because both are how we will build the most bridges possible.

As Kim and I got to know each other better, we prayed a few times together. I remember one day when she was struggling, I asked if we could pray, right there, at the bus stop. Our kids were already on the bus and I could tell by the tears in her eyes what she shared weighed heavy on her heart. I know prayers lifts burdens because it transfers the weight off of us and onto Jesus. My neighbor was hurting. I didn't ask her to come into my church to pray. We prayed where the need was, which was at the bus stop. I did invite her to my church, but what was more important is that we experienced God together, organically, where the need was.

Evangelist and author Oswald Chambers said, "We have to pray with our eyes on God, not on the difficulties." Any time and place is a good one to help our friends get their eyes off the difficulties and on God.

I love my church family (if you're in the Virginia/Washington DC area, come visit us The Life Church http://welovechurch.com/), but I don't need to be inside the church building to experience God. God is omnipresent. Everywhere. We're His ambassadors, and need to go everywhere to tell others about Christ. The sad part is only 2% of Christians in America share their faith on a regular basis.[1]

Why is this? Where have we gone wrong in deciding to hide our faith? I know I could try to blame others, or media or some subversive agenda, but I have got to own my own actions and decide who I'll serve: my fear of other's rejecting me or the Lord.

For years, this was my pattern: meet people, invite/bring them to church and let the smart church folks do the rest. See how easy it is to become a comfortable spectator (consumer) of Christianity instead of a get in the game kind of contributor?

The year I met Kim was the year I began my inspirational speaking career. I really didn't know if it was going to be a "career", but I stepped out in faith and experimented. Four months before we met at the neighborhood Super Bowl party, Kim was at one of my speaking engagements, which was for a mom's group and inside a church building. God was already laying the bridge building groundwork inside of a church building to continue constructing outside the church walls before we officially became friends.

I'm a human BEing, not a human DOer. I can do, but I can't forget to be. God awoke in me the idea/thought to do AND be available for service inside and outside the church. I didn't adjust enough margin time to just "be" and have hang time. Often in those "be" moments is where organic God-moments and relationship occur, like praying at the bus stop. I believe bridges are built one plank, stone, and relationship at a time.

A missional church is a church that defines itself, and organizes its life around, its real purpose as an agent of God's mission to the world.[2] Truly, when Christians are told in Matthew 22:39 to *love your neighbors as yourself*, it's bigger than just our street. We commonly think of neighbors as the people who live near us, but Jesus meant it to include all mankind–even our enemies! Jesus told His famous parable of the Good Samaritan to make it clear that "love your neighbor" means to love all persons, everywhere–not just our friends, allies, countrymen.[3]

Here's the thing. I told you I was the first woman elected to my church Board of Directors in over 25 years. I took my position seriously. I seriously considered doing what was normal practice for past board members. You could only have three consecutive one-year terms and then have to take the fourth year off. I considered doing this because I vacillated: Would I be letting women down by not accepting the nomination? More importantly would I be letting God down?

I'm a person who is very serious about my love of and service for Jesus. So serious that sometimes I can get handcuffed to a church job for a host of very well intentioned reasons. Maybe you're feeling stuck in a church position knowing you're doing great work and don't want to leave your position because you think, "There's no one else to fill this position." Or, "We've advertised and no one is stepping up. I can't leave a gap." Or, "If I don't do it, who will?"

Pray, pray and pray some more. If God is closing this season of service, it's for a very great reason. Maybe someone needs to see the need and rise up to the job. Or maybe that position just needs to stay empty and allow God to adjust the ministry, needs or more importantly, hearts.

I love the visual reminder found in Matthew 9:17 how God doesn't pour new wine in old wineskins. New wine is poured into new wineskins. What this means is that when Jesus brings a "new something" it can't be confined or contained within the old! God doesn't change, but how He chooses to use us does change!

I will always find different ways to serve within and outside my church walls. In fact, it was through serving on the church board where we read and discussed *The Forgotten Ways* by missionologist Alan Hirsh. This is where I first read the staggering statistic how about 60% of Americans will no longer come inside the church walls. Meaning, more than half of Americans are not going to come into the church building. This means one thing. We're going to have to go to them. We'll cover the "go" part in the last chapter, but for now, suffice to say, we do need to "go"!

As I look at the state of the world today, I see there are a lot of bridge building opportunities. Building bridges and following Jesus involves adventure. I no longer want to live isolated solely within church walls, but rather adventure in and out of the church building.

Don't get me wrong, I felt like I did do good work while I sat on the board, but I felt the Lord had shifted my focus to "and"; in and out. Not just one, both.

There are critical bridge building opportunities everywhere we go independent of whether we're inside or outside the church building. We can always do something more to step up and reach outside the church while also reaching out to newcomers inside the church building. All interactions make the kingdom grow! We need to be the church and build bridges in and out for God's glory.

*Name changed to protect privacy.

Discussion Questions

1. Journal/share your thoughts on this chapter.

2. Where do you feel most comfortable–inside or outside the church building walls? Why do you feel most comfortable there?

3. Do you feel like you're effectively building bridges inside AND outside or is it "or"? How do you change the "or" to an "and"?

4. When have you ever felt "it", like a hypocrite?

5. Who did God mean when He declared, *"Love your neighbor?"*

6. Are there any exceptions or limitations to the word "neighbor" for you?

7. How do you feel about sharing your faith with neighbors? Are you worried about offending them?

8. Have you ever struggled letting go of a position because you wondered, "There's no one else to fill the role?" When and what role?

9. What are your thoughts on Jake's analogy, "Church is like the locker room, the world is like the football game"? Have you ever been hurt by being out on the playing field?

Chapter 5

UNLEASHED

Forgiven people, forgive people. Rick Warren

I sat in my home office and peered above my laptop screen at the beautiful pond. I took so many brain-breaks there. Moments later, he walked in front of the pond with his unleashed Rottweiler dog. His dog was unleashed, *again*.

We live in a Home Owners Association (HOA) community where there are certain rules established which we are all expected to follow. We have rules where/when you can put your trashcans out, how you can/can't maintain your yard and another stating you need to have your dog leashed. I am freely admitting I am an "HOA Pharisee" about this rule. I love dogs. Remember, I bring mine, *leashed*, to play tennis where I'm not supposed to?

I don't care if you have a teacup poodle or a Rottweiler; I want your pooch leashed. It's not only a safety issue, it's also a community hygiene issue. If your dog's not leashed and poops, how do you know where to pick up your dog's poop? Right? Right.

Countless times I saw this man and his unleashed dog frolic in front of my window and I'd think, "So not cool, man."

Weeks later, my kids and I played outside with neighborhood friends. We live in suburbia where lush grass blades are limited and sidewalks are abundant. We had a great time outside until the man and his unleashed dog walked toward us.

Let me give you a little back-story as to why this man and his unleashed dog doubly stressed me out. As you now know, I don't like dogs running unleashed in my hood. The second reason is my across the street neighbor, *Deena, was outside with her two children. They are afraid of dogs.

Deena and I shared not just a street, we shared a mutual passion for both our faith and family. We helped one another out. I helped her kids with their homework. Deena had difficulty reading and writing because English wasn't her first language. They didn't have a home computer and some of her daughter's assignments needed a computer. I was eager to share our computer.

Deena was equally eager to help. When my husband was injured during his night fire duty crew shift, Deena quickly came over to stay with my kids who were asleep. She stayed with my kids, so I could be with Dave at the hospital.

Their family had one vehicle and her husband left early for work, so I'd let her borrow my sexy minivan. Please, I drive a minivan, let me live in the delusion of adding such an adjective before my mode of transportation. Thank you.

Deena had an obvious desire to convert me to Islam. If faith conversion was a sport, I'd rank my homegirl in the professional level. Deena was persistent; passed me Islam pamphlets about Muhammad (tracts) and had a prophet hierarchy poster in her dining room that she referred to regularly during our conversations. I knew anytime she led me into her dining room it was to highlight the prophet chart, again.

She thoughtfully included my family in her celebration of Ramadan, the Islamic holiday celebrated by fasting from sun up to sun down. When she broke her fast at night, she'd often ring my doorbell and share her handmade specialty celebratory food, which was way better than my cooking.

We'd often have lengthy discussions and she'd tell me, "Jesus was a good man, but only a good man. Allah is higher, better." Our conversations would almost certainly circle around to what we could agree on, "God is love". She didn't believe I needed "three gods" and while I tried, miserably so, to explain the Trinity is actually One, my words didn't resonate and I decided I stunk at evangelism.

Well, my evangelism efforts were about to get worse.

Through our friendship, I learned about some of the things that she found important like a clean home and collecting perfume. I also learned some of her religious practices, which included prayer, covering her head and neck, not talking to men who were not her husband and not touching a dog. She considered a dog's saliva "unclean". This is where her and her children's dog fear came from. They wanted to adhere to their religious rules.

We had two dogs at the time, Romeo and Juliet, so I kept them away from her, the best I could, to respect her belief. I don't have to agree with her rule to honor her rule.

Back to the man and his unleashed dog...

Deena and her kids were also outside the day when the man and his unleashed dog walked toward us. Her oldest daughter ran toward home in fear.

I decided to stand up for my neighbor, her convictions and let's face it, my mounting irritation. Deena was a very assertive woman, but her religion told her not to talk to this man because he wasn't her husband.

Very nicely, I called out, "Sir, can you please put your dog on a leash?"

He curtly responded, "My dog is trained, he doesn't need a leash."

Uh, oh. Game on. This dude just poked a ghetto-fabulous-born-and-raised-New-Jersey-girl-bear.

The dude then called his dog over to him. His dog ignored him and walked farther away from him.

Sarcastic Steph appeared, "I can see he's well-trained. Can you please put your dog on a leash? It is the law and my friend and some children are afraid."

"Well then have your friend ask me herself."

Oh. No. He. Did. Not.

What I needed to do was keep calm and build a bridge.

What I needed to do is remember love builds bridges.

What I needed to do is bridge a gap.

What I needed to do is sing, "Jesus take the wheel!"

What I needed to be is an ambassador for Christ.

What I needed to do is chilleth outeth.

But oh, no. The crazy train left the station. As steam tooted out of my ears, I walked toward him and prayed I still remembered the pressure points learned in my law-enforcement academy because I was ready to scrap. "She doesn't have to ask you because I just did. Put your dog on a leash. Now."

Let me assure you the dog wasn't the only thing unleashed at this point.

"They have nothing to be afraid of. My dog is trained."

The dude went on to explain how Rottweiler's were misunderstood, not aggressive and had been given a bad reputation. I explained this had nothing do to with the type of dog and every-thing to do with other people and the community rules. I added, "If your dog was trained, then he would've come when you called him. Put your dog on leash or I'm calling the cops."

When I went inside my home that afternoon I felt like a complete failure as a Christian. I wasn't patient or kind. I allowed myself to get unhinged, unleashed and blew up, bad. I didn't want Deena or my other neighbors, two of who were actively considering deeper levels of Christianity, to think

Christians acted like the way I behaved. But we do. We fall. I fell in a disrespectful yelling match with my neighbor. I forgot all about how I needed to keep calm and build a bridge and that I need to lead with love, not my ginormous attitude.

Later that week, I walked Romeo and Juliet, and noticed "him" and his leashed dog. I felt a specific conviction to apologize to him. I've learned when the direction is a specific conviction, it's the Holy Spirit guiding. When it's a general guilt, it's the devil. So, God and I had a little discussion. I bartered, "Okay God, if I see him at the cross block, I will apologize."

I hoped I wouldn't see him. Minutes later, we intersected.

As we approached on opposite sides of the street, I uncomfortably spoke, "I want to apologize for the way I talked to you earlier this week. I don't ever want to talk to a neighbor the way I talked to you and I hope you will forgive me."

The man looked up at me, his shoulders dropped (my presence clearly made him tense), and replied, "I feel really bad too. My name is *Ron would you forgive me too?"

I realized it's not *if* we fail and fall as Christians, we will fail and fall. It's much more about how we allow God to deal with us and pick us back up shows the world about whom we love.

After this day, every time we passed each other, Ron and I exchanged friendly greetings.

I desperately want to tell you I never saw his dog unleashed again, but I did. And yes, it irritated me. And no, I never did call the cops.

When the moments were right, I told Deena and the other neighborhood friends that I asked Ron for forgiveness for the way I talked to him. I was even uncomfortable then, each time I shared about my apologizing to Ron with my neighborhood friends.

Do you know why it was so uncomfortable for me? I'm ridiculously proud. Pride is a sin (Proverbs 8:13). Any sin distances me from intimacy with God and others.

After I learned a few Bible verses and stories, I got puffy proud (Psalm 10:4). I really like and prefer being right. You know who else got puffy proud and didn't like being wrong? The Pharisees. Jesus corrected the Pharisees because they were so puffy proud there was no room for the Lord to be the Lord in their lives and beautiful love to bloom. Their self-proclaimed righteousness and strict adherence to being holy in their own eyes is what made them in fact unholy. The Pharisees hid behind the own perceived "good performance" and adherence to God's laws. They didn't understand God's not impressed with a flawless performance; He wants your heart to be fully devoted and reliant on Him. This means when we fall, as I did with Ron, we run toward Him and His humble ways. Not puff up and get our performance perfected so we can then come to God. God accepts and loves broken and imperfect people. And friend, I'm so grateful.

I know God wants me to be more concerned with being humble than being right. I can't even begin to tell you how many times I wanted to be right when Dave and I have had an argument. Not only do I want to be right, the delusional side of me wants to be celebrated for being oh, so right. I know it's delusional, but I'm being honest here. The Holy Spirit meets me in my delusion and regularly speaks this statement into me, "Be more concerned with being humble, than being right." Humility grows relationships. Pride shrinks relationships.

My relationship to my husband is the most intimate human relationship I have. When we disagree, I so often struggle with wanting to be right because I like being right. And, far too many times, I dig my feet in, pour cement around and become stuck; immoveable in my right-ness, in my own self proclaimed righteousness. The times I've let go of my need to be right, Right, RIGHT!, I've also experience not only our resolution occur quicker, our intimacy is restored in a much more beautiful way.

I know God's a patient parent committed to my growth and development because He loves me and has a great plan for my life. It's uncomfortable to decrease in puffiness so God can increase in power, yet so necessary. It's vital to decrease so God can increase in all areas of my life and relationships.

The truth is that God opposes proud people and gives grace to the humble (James 4:6). God's grace resides in humility. The most humble leader I've ever known was Jesus. Sure, He got righteously angry (Matthew 21:12-13), but He never got puffy proud. When I reflect on Jesus' life, the life I truly want to emulate, I see Jesus did not choose comfort or convenience; Jesus chose conviction.

I'm convinced and convicted the world needs more unleashed apologies than unleashed attitude. We need more grace, truth, love and forgiveness. Especially when we feel a tad more right. Just because a dog and his owner are unleashed doesn't justify or give me permission to unleash a disrespectful attitude. Two wrongs do not make a right.

I need, all Christians need to lead with love and unleash an apology. When we apologize and ask for forgiveness to others and to God because Mark 11:26 says, *so that your Father in heaven may forgive you your sins.*

Rick Warren simply states, "Forgiven people forgive people." My friends, what Christ did for you and me on the cross-said we are unleashed, free and forgiven. This means I put a leash on my pride and unleash my gratitude remembering just how much Jesus has forgiven me. It means I lower myself down to actual size and not get too puffy proud. It does not mean I become apathetic because I think I'm a little bit more right or know a couple more Bible verses. It means I put Bible verses like *love my neighbor* (Mark 12:31) into action. It means I don't just read, *Love my neighbor*; I actually love my neighbor: the one with the untrained and unleashed dog, the Muslim one, the spiritually seeking ones, the one who was suicidal in a local bookstore, the one who had an abortion, the one who wrote hate mail to the girl who had an abortion, the one who brought her dog to the tennis court, the one who told the woman to not bring her dog to the tennis court. Let's start right where we live. Let's love those neighbors.

When I finally understood that accepting Jesus as my Savior means that He forgave my past and died just for me, I wept. When I understood, not just academically but experientially what Jesus did for me, I felt humbled, grateful and challenged. Challenged to let go of my own personal comfort and stride closer to my convictions, to be less Steph like and more Christ like.

Jesus told a story in Matthew 18:21-35 about an employee who had an enormous debt equivalent to about $10,000,000 in today's currency. He could not repay his boss, so he pled for forgiveness. His boss had mercy and forgave his entire debt. Not soon after, the very same employee had a coworker who owed the employee money. Mind you, it was a significant amount less than the debt the employee was just released from, about $17.00.[1] The employee forgot about his boss' generosity. The employee aggressively demanded payment from his coworker. When the boss found out what happened, he went crazy and had the employee placed in jail until he paid his debt. The story closes with a sharp reminder that if we don't forgive others, this is how God will treat us.

Jesus forgives our debts we'll never be able to repay. Not only do we need to forgive others, we need to ask for forgiveness from God and others.

A well-placed apology is humbling, sometimes uncomfortable and most like Christ. I know it's uncomfortable. I know you'd rather not feel so vulnerable. When we unleash a well-placed and meaningful apology, what we're doing is building a bridge, using the stones thrown at us, or the stones we've thrown, as building blocks. We need to use those stones to build a bridge out, not a wall up.

When we ask for forgiveness, walls of hate, hurt and animosity get broken down and those very same stones can be used to build a bridge of love and connection.

My son's friend, the same friend that has "refrigerator and put-your-own-dishes-in-the-dishwasher privileges" in our home, once told me, "Miss Stephanie, you remind me of my gym teacher." He said this because I'm regularly found in either running shorts or yoga pants because I am a big fan of comfort. I'm all about the comfort of hats too because they're convenient to hide bed head.

There's nothing wrong with enjoying comforts and conveniences and I do: I sleep in a Sleep Number® bed. I can go from "TV watching chill" mode to "flat sleeping" mode in the push of one comfortable button. I have a single cup coffee brewer which I've named Java the Hut, because I'm odd and because I like hot, fresh coffee, when I want hot, fresh coffee. The seats in my husband's car have both heating and cooling modes. I love riding in his car because I love being at the most comfortable temperature no matter the season. There's nothing wrong with enjoying comforts and conveniences as long as they do not rule us. I am naturally drawn toward comfort and convenience, so much so that I often choose my own comfort and convenience over my convictions. God doesn't want comfortable consumers of the Gospel; He wants committed contributors.

My friends, building bridges is often not comfortable or convenient. Building bridges isn't just turning the other cheek and building. There are many factors that must be taken into consideration. Comfort and convenience are not the top factors; conviction to follow Christ is.

Some bridges, for one reason or another, will never be built. You might have the courage and conviction, but there are other factors in the equation like other people's choices.

I felt discouraged about a situation where I tried building a bridge, a bridge I knew God asked me to build, but I'm still at square one. On the outside, it's not looking very good at all. After numerous attempts, the puffy proud part of me wanted to build up a tall wall to comfortably avoid rejection and yet God told me to wait. Do not build up or out. Just wait. Be patient.

As you stride and struggle building bridges, remember this: obedience is my job; the outcomes are God's job. God rewards obedience and it's not based on the responses of others. Let's live and work for the applause of One. Sure, I hope there are successful bridges built, but when and if there aren't, remember you are God's child. God loves you. Remember for whom you live and work. Keep focused on the last thing God told you to do and be faithful even when you don't hear any applause.

If someone burns a bridge you built, that's between God and the other person. Don't let one burnt bridge distract you and justify apathy. Don't build a wall up. Get over the issue you had with this person. Keep building where God says so. And, be patient with yourself and others.

What the world needs to see is the evidence of God alive in us. There's a connecting bridge made when God's character attributes: love, joy, peace, forbearance, kindness, goodness, faithfulness, gentleness and self-control (Galatians 5:22-23) are evident in our actions.

Sometimes I'd rather not go hang out with people who are a little different than me because it can be uncomfortable and inconvenient. Remember, God puts different people in our lives to help us not be the same. Being around different people helps fortify our faith and to mature us as believers and friends. I'd never know that Muslims don't want to pet a dog if I didn't have some as friends.

Something I want us both to keep remembering is that who we are today is not who we'll be forever! We are capable of growing and evolving all because of God's rich truth and grace. God transforms us. I am not the same woman I was 20 years ago, when I gave my heart and life to Jesus in a San Antonio, Texas church. I'm not the same woman who wrote Tina a hate note or told off Ron.

God has a vision for my life and it's greater than the sum of my mistakes and successes as of today. This vision is revealed through relationships and circumstances with God and others.

Jesus brings me comfort. When it's painfully clear I need to be more humble, and a lot less of a jerk to my neighbor, Jesus envelops me with His love and grace. He reminds me that's it's human to miss the mark, blow up at my neighbor, or find it difficult to apologize. But, with His strength, I recover and pick myself back up. Humility bridges hearts together.

God's vision for His people is so much bigger than we can imagine. He's my parent and cares about me, all parts of me. I'm a parent. Most days, I could see beyond my child's temper tantrum and knew they would learn how to walk and talk. I still have a vision for their adult lives and it is awesome! On a much grander scale, my

Heavenly Father has a bigger vision for you and me. It's way bigger than our today!

When I reflect on Jesus' life, the life I truly want to emulate, I see Jesus did not choose comfort or convenience, Jesus chose conviction.

I believe Jesus modeled conviction through living in a community He intentionally built. This is where He shared life, spoke truth, gave grace and replicated love.

I believe all people long for meaningful community where they can be safe to share their strengths and weaknesses without fear of being judged and criticized.

I believe real community has the comfort of and the conviction to speak truth, apologize and be forgiven. It's living a lifestyle of patient surrender and forgiveness to God, self and others, based on a remembering of Who forgives us.

Community is where our strengths and weaknesses are identified. God wants us to live in communion with Him and He brings the community where we learn more about Him, others and even ourselves. I learned how impatient and proud I am in my neighborhood community. I also learned how sensitive I am for the overlooked.

God identifies gaps in us and in the world and we glimpse the bigger vision God has for us. In time, others will see Who the true Gap-Filler is, and God will get the glory because love (God) covers gaps (1 Peter 4:8).

New York Times Best-Selling author of *Love Does*, Bob Goff, wrote, "If we're satisfied doing what we're used to, it'll be to miss what we've been made for." If we remain leashed to our comfort, we'll never unleash our purpose! When we decide to let go of our comforts in order to stretch towards our faith convictions, God will use us to unleash apologies, grace and purposeful bridge building.

*Names changed to protect privacy.

Discussion Questions:

1. Journal/share your thoughts on this chapter.

2. Can you think of a time when someone sincerely apologized to you? Recall the details and what meant most to you. How did you feel before and after?

3. Recall a time when you needed to apologize to another person. What were the events that led up to the apology? How did you feel before and after?

4. What are some of your favorite comforts and conveniences?

5. Is there any way you have chosen comfort over conviction? This may be good and this may be bad. Evaluate and share.

6. When is a time you chose conviction over comfort? Share the details.

7. What are your thoughts about, "Obedience is my job and outcome is God's job?"

Chapter 6

THE GAP

I've learned that people will forget what you said, people will forget what you did, but people will never forget how you made them feel.
Maya Angelou

I stood in my bathroom and applied mascara when *Lynn walked in and with tear-filled eyes said, "I'm scared to go back to church. Last time I went, they kicked me out."

I didn't know her church, the people there or exactly what they said, but I do know how they made my loved one feel. Not good enough. Less than. Flawed. Unwanted. Thrown out.

I pulled her close and promised, "If someone gives you a hard time (at my church), they will deal with me." We both shed more tears and Lynn trembled. She trembled in my arms. After suffering through this rejection, she stopped going to church altogether.

We've already identified the gap that 60% of Americans won't come into a church building. I see this gap as a widening gap and in desperate need of repair bridgework.

Churches are often advertised as "safe" places, except Lynn didn't feel safe at hers. Countless times, I've heard Christians refer to churches (meaning the building here) as "hospitals for sick people who need a healer (Jesus)." But I've seen a gap from what is preached to what is reality. When certain patients are denied care and admission into "the hospital", there is a gap, which must be addressed.

We're all patients, with varied wounds, in need of a healer. The healer's name is Jesus. Jesus is inclusive. When Christians behave in an exclusive rather than an inclusive manner, we need to adjust our efforts to fill these exclusive gaps with unconditional love as Jesus does for us. If we only allow "certain people" inside the church building hospital, then we're not reflecting Jesus. We're reflecting something entirely different, possibly our self-obsessed preferences.

You may be wondering why my loved one was kicked out of her church. She told her church leaders that she was a homosexual. They decided to kick her out of the hospital. They decided that they would only let certain sinners, who had certain sins, into the hospital.

Now before you think I'm judging those church leaders, I want you to know I have a huge heart for church leaders. I know the pressures and joys of being a church leader. I've held a variety of church leadership positions: elder, board member, bible study leader, nursery ministry leader, inmate mentor, and Vacation Bible Study teacher. I reach thousands of people weekly through my Encouraged in Heart speaking engagements, blog posts and social media venues. I'm a former military officer and know that any kind of leadership position is a double-edged privilege and burden. Leaders influence and impact other lives and we need to pray for and not judge our leaders (1 Timothy 2:1-4). Let me say this one more time. We need to pray for, not judge, our leaders. Prayer bridges gaps.

Before I get "ready to rumble" about Lynn's former church leader's gaps, I need to work on my own gaps. When you have the courage to stop criticizing other people's shortcomings and focus on your own, God gives you power. Remember, God opposes proud people (self-first) and gives abundant grace and favor to the humble (God-first) folks (James 4:6).

I recently saw a gigantic gap in myself as I scrolled through and judged my Facebook "friends". Within two minutes, I scrolled through at least 50 status updates and thought one judgmental thought after the next: "Cute!" "Ridiculous." "Yeah, that person's a Christian... not." "Hilarious." "Give me a break, you're not that holy." "Cover up, would ya?" "Wow, so profound." "I wish we were closer." "Thank God we're not closer."

I'm not free to love more like Christ when I'm chained to critical judgment of other people. Judging lengthens the gap to where I'm only in a position and distance to observe. When the gap is shortened, now we're close enough to talk and have meaningful heart exchanges. When the gap is widened, there's often loud communications that take place to cover the distance and get "heard"; the wider the gap the more difficult it is to both share and hear.

Sure, we're to use wisdom and ask the Holy Spirit for discernment, but not judge others. I judged a neighbor whose dog regularly barked outdoors and I wondered, "Why don't they bring the dog in more?" (What is it with dogs and me?)

After I got to know the neighbors and some of their stories, I not only thoroughly enjoy being around them, I found their beloved old dog is incontinent and piddles in the house. They put her outside so she piddles outside. As you well know by now, I've had more than one neighborhood dog lesson. After you hear someone's story, no matter how short or long, you have an inside glimpse into their heart. Listen intently. People normally give clues as to what's most important to them and often it takes active listening to learn what is most important *to them*. Listening bridges gaps. When we listen we learn the "why" to their cry, the file (the reasons) behind their smile and in the right time, we can share God's glory in our own story.

Listening to someone's story changes two hearts. Where there's understanding, I did not write total agreement, hearts soften and gaps shorten. Now when I hear my neighbor's dog bark, it has minimal effect on me because I think my neighbors are awesome. I understand some of their "why" and learned they want their dog and living conditions more comfortable.

But what about the people I feel unable to relate to? How do we bridge these gaps with strangers and people in our everyday life?

One day, my kids were getting on my last nerve. Then my husband called and asked me to pick something up at Home Depot. Not only did I not want to run the errand, I also did not feel like (maturely) parenting my kids.

Every once in a while I get a good idea. This was one of those rare moments. As we drove to Home Depot, I told my boys we were going to have a competition once at Home Depot. Whoever got the most strangers to smile back at them while at Home Depot, wins. I knew this would get their attention because let's just say they get their competitive natures honestly.

As we redirected our energy outward and smiled at strangers, the day's stress lifted. Smiling makes you feel happy! I lost count at how many people smiled back at my offspring and who won because we had so much fun! When you're out walking your (leashed) dog or passing a coworker's desk, make genuine eye contact and smile. Cheerfulness bridges gaps.

You may be wondering, "Well, how do I do this? Give me some more examples." Okay, don't mind if I do. I had a bridge built to me as I worshiped next to a newer friend, *Andrea, at a large women's conference. The worship lyrics said "You (God) make me brave" and I busted into tears because at that moment I didn't feel brave. I was actually in the middle of this book project and wanted to shrink back. My friend reached over and held my hand. No words. She didn't say anything; she just showed up. She built a bridge toward my heart by touching my hand and it touched my heart. She didn't have to know all the details; she just genuinely cared. Compassion bridges gaps.

You can build bridges even if you're sitting on your child's sports field sidelines. One season, I built a bridge to another athlete's parent by listening to her tearfully share about her marriage. I briefly shared about when my hubby and I separated to empathize with her pain, but didn't monopolize the conversation and give a "my pain was worse than your current pain." Empathy bridges gaps.

Different seasons bring different bridge building opportunities to shorten gaps. As you mow your lawn or shovel your snow, chat with your neighbors. If they had surgery, are away on work travel or have a newborn, shovel or mow their lawn to bless them. Kindness bridges gaps.

If you're picking up a coffee in route to work, recognize what your coworker likes to drink and pick one up for him or her. While making some chicken noodle soup or lasagna, make a double portion. Ask God to show you who could use the meal. Thoughtfulness bridges gaps.

When the Apostle Paul bridged gaps, he got radical. This is a dude who knew how to lead with love, unleash God's love, suffer for the

Gospel and build bridges. Paul loved non-Christian people so much that he modified his life to become like them. When he went to the Jews, he followed the laws the Jews obeyed (1 Corinthians 9:19-23). He said he was free, but made himself a slave to everyone for the purpose to win as many as possible for Jesus. He didn't have to, he chose to. He didn't change his faith; he changed his approach and methods with how to effectively share his faith. My friend, Pastor Brad Russell, said, "Compromise your method, not your message." Adapting your methods (not your message!) bridges gaps.

When Paul went to Greece, he changed his approach yet again and spoke in Greek. He didn't speak Hebrew there because they spoke (and still speak) Greek. Paul communicated and related in a way that's meaningful to people he was interested and invested in sharing the Gospel. Paul modified his approach with the heart to reach the people he loved to tell them God loves them. He understood his role as God's ambassador. He wanted to receive the blessings a life with Christ has to offer.

One day, I stood in the airport check in line and noticed the tween girl behind me reading

Divergent. I had just read *Divergent* in my book club so I had something to talk with her about. I'm not pretending to be a tween (that'd be a sinking ship!); I'm just relating to the tween leveraging our commonality. Identifying commonality bridges gaps.

The day I talked to the tween about *Divergent* I wouldn't have talked to her about benefits for military veterans. She would have thought, "What do I care about military veteran benefits?" I quickly studied her and found a way to begin relating with her in a way that's relatable and relevant to her. Being relevant bridges gaps.

I love it when my pastor, David Baird, says; "I'll do anything short of sin, to win someone for Christ." He's not advertising living a sloppy or sub-standard life, quite the opposite. He's saying it's time to let go of comfort. The Gospel demands its followers to be warriors and get in the game!

If God leads you to read a youth fiction book like *Divergent* to better able to relate to the younger generation, then do it!

A young woman I mentor, *Marie, likes to chat online. I never Google chatted before her. For the record, I do not like to chat online. I think there are more efficient ways to communicate, but I went with the flow because I sensed a bigger purpose. A lot of the younger generation prefers this method of communication. Texting, too. If chatting online was her preference, I can adapt my communication preference because I'm shooting for her heart and I'm not offending God or God's ways doing so. I can surely adapt.

There were some things Marie needed to share chatting on line. By "things" I mean sin. She was ashamed and chatting on line made it safer for her to share about her porn addiction and sex life. I didn't like what she shared, because it grieved God's heart and mine too, but I buckled in and read/listened/replied. After a few months of connecting, talking and chatting on line, she had a desire to release certain sins and behaviors, get baptized and is now in a very intimate relationship with Christ. She's currently getting her masters in Bible Studies. We almost never chat online anymore because through the years, we've bridged some gaps. We have trust and comfort built and poured a loved foundation. The online chatting was her then preference not her now preference. Communicating in a relevant way builds trust and bridges gaps.

Study the people around you and examine what makes them tick, what their preferences are. As long as it doesn't cause you to sin or compromise what you know is right, go for it! Your building style won't be the same as you bridge toward your coworker, to tween to neighbor. So when the Holy Spirit prompts you to build in a new way or different way (remember the bookstore), remember that He made all His kids different for a purpose!

Bringing a coworker a coffee or listening to someone may seem like surface stuff, but remember, we need to get through the surface "stuff" to get to the heart. And after all's said and done, the heart is what we're shooting for. It takes time and patience to bridge gaps and get to heart matters.

Many church leaders are wisely addressing the gap in the corporate church attendance decline by adapting their methods with the heart to reach the younger generation and today's visually stimulating culture. I've observed so many Christian hearts that have hardened and considered their own comforts to be a higher priority than reaching non-Christian and younger generation hearts. Then, not so ironically, these are often the same people who piously state their disapproval of society and in the "youth of today."

When we fail to lead and invest in our youth and society, we can take the blame. Whether we want to face it or not, we are leading the younger generation. If we continue in a mentality of "this is how we've always done church and experienced God, so they can take it or leave it"–the younger generation is often choosing the latter option. They're leaving it. And it's our fault for not leaving our preferences behind to bridge toward our younger generation; you know the same people who will be pushing our wheelchairs and leading our churches and country. Don't be afraid to adapt your methods such as worship style and visual aids to meet the younger generation. It's our honor and duty to lead them. Don't change your God-centered message, but do adapt your methods to ensure the message gets heard.

The culture today is not the same culture as when Jesus walked the earth. To effectively meet today's culture and youth, we need to adapt our methods, not our message. Christ is compelling, but some of our methods of how we worship and celebrate Christ aren't compelling. Bridge the generational and cultural gaps by adapting your methods, but never your Christ-centered message.

I served on the church Board of Directors with a Vietnam veteran named *Eddie. He's such a good guy. Eddie has a gruff exterior and a teddy bear interior. He didn't fool me with exterior because I shot for the heart and heard his heart. He does not like nor prefer the worship style of his church. He does, however, like and believe in reaching the younger generation as he volunteers in the children's ministry and wears ear plugs during worship. He's not compromised the message, but he has compromised his methods and remains a true war and faith hero in my book.

There are so many gaps. Not just gaps within church buildings, there are gaps within the church. The church is not a building; the church is Christ's people. And there are gaps in how Christians, "the church", live out their faith.

I see glaring contradictions when gluttons like me are welcomed into Christian churches to sin and binge eat. Yet others with different sins or issues that need support and healing aren't as welcomed into the church "hospital". Wherever there is sin, there is healing that is needed. Jesus and community are the treatment. When people are denied from the Jesus community, then where will they go to find healing for their pain? They often make more pain for themselves in their attempts to alleviate their pain.

I've observed a lot of gaps in the treatment of certain groups of people. These are just some of the people I've seen overlooked and marginalized by Christians, people who: are divorced, have mental illness, suffer with depression, are a single parent, are recovering from abortions, are the "wrong color/class/political affiliation", identify as homosexual/bisexual and transgendered and have tattoos and piercings. There are a lot more gaps; I just wanted to mention a few here. You see, when some friends, like Lynn, aren't as openly welcomed, I see IT. What if Lynn was your child? Wouldn't you pray and hope for your child to be welcomed into a Jesus community and loved and encouraged into a deeper relationship with Christ? And, just in case you wondered, Lynn did feel welcomed at our church. She also thought it was cool that there was a female drummer in the worship team.

I believe how we respond to different people tells more about our own maturity than the

Jesus we say we love. You don't have to be like others to love them. We're often not comfortable around "different" and long for same-ness. Jesus didn't invest in people who were just like Him. Christians need to study Jesus' ways. He invested in all and different kinds of people. Jesus cared for, touched and healed lepers, who were society's outcasts, when the "religious folks" wouldn't dare to do such a thing (Matthew 8:2-3).

God doesn't make cookie cutter Christians. Jesus wants us to accept and love the people, not the sins. I love this cartoon for a ton of reasons. It captures IT so well and challenges to love wider and bridge better!

COOKIE CUTTER CHRISTIANS? A Joyful 'toon by Mike Waters

Accept one another, then just as Christ accepted you, in order to bring praise to God. – Romans 15:7

There's a world out there, inside and outside our church walls, filled with non-Christians. Many of whom believe Christians don't care enough about them and are judgmental toward them. And, like my loved one, they don't just perceive this in their imagination; they experience it firsthand.

Many times our words say that we will *love our neighbor* (Mark 12:31), but our actions reveal a gap that, "I will love only some neighbors where it's comfortable or socially acceptable." We've already covered this, but it's worth mentioning again: we all struggle with something. We all need Jesus. Don't make or widen a gap when certain groups of strugglers aren't allowed or denied admission into the hospital. Often the ones who are denied admission are the ones that actually need to be in the ICU and ministered to with intensive care.

I desperately want the "church people" to be safe people who are beacons of God's unconditional and patient love. I didn't write perfect because perfection is off the table because perfection is not possible this side of Heaven.

This change starts with you and me, one relationship (plank) at a time. How will people ever know Jesus loves them unless we reflect that love in our own lives? We must identify with them, bridge gaps and demonstrate love versus judgment and criticism. Stop focusing on how different someone is and look for something you have in common and build from there. Again, I did not write, "agree", I wrote, "identify" with.

Sometimes we're going to have to tell people we love them. More powerfully, we need our actions to scream we love them way louder than our words. Actions speak louder than words. One of the ways we do this is we invite people into our lives no matter if we're comfortable, familiar, like or not like them.

As bridge builders, it's your and my job to make sure others know we do care. When someone is different than us, it is not the time to build a bridge and get over him or her. It's time to build a bridge over the gap and get to them, the hearts that need to know other people care and share the hope of Christ.

Now is the time to be building bridges and close the gap caused by isolation and indifference. Now is the time for compassion and salvation. Now is the time to bridge gaps.

I'm not even going to begin to suggest I have this all figured out, because I don't. Most days I have more questions than answers. But what I do know is there are some gaps in the people that label themselves as Christians. There are gaps in people like me. I want God to use me to help bridge those gaps in a most imperfect and earnest way.

In his book, *Out of Solitude: Three Meditations on the Christian Life*, author Henri J.M. Nouwen captures bridging gaps in such a beautiful way, "When we honestly ask ourselves which person in our lives mean the most to us, we often find that it is those who, instead of giving advice, solutions, or cures, have chosen rather to share our pain and touch our wounds with a warm and tender hand. The friend who can be silent with us in a moment of despair or confusion, who can stay with us in an hour of grief and bereavement, who can tolerate not knowing, not curing, not healing and face with us the reality of our powerlessness, that is a friend who cares."

Compassion, listening, acceptance (not of the sin, but of the person – there is a distinct difference) and love narrow the gaps. People won't consider whatever you're offering, even if it's free and awesome, if they don't feel safe. I'm not saying lose your standards, I'm saying don't let your standards create more gaps.

I want to be a safe person. Sometimes I am, and other times, I'm not. I desperately want the "church people" to be safe people. This starts with you and me, one gap bridging relationship at a time.

Don't let disagreements discourage or distract your bridge building efforts. We have to mature past having to agree with everyone about everything. (Respectful) Disagreements can be awesome springboards into knowing others more and them knowing you, and your Jesus, better.

Be prepared to give a reason for the joy and hope you have, but the end part of 1 Peter 3:15 says to do so with gentleness and respect. I believe we should disagree in the same manner we share, with gentleness and respect. We need to be more eager to listen to others and less eager to talk and become angry (James 1:19).

Data collected by the General Social Survey, which has tracked the behavior and attitudes of Americans for the last four decades, found "One out of four people don't have anyone in their lives who gets them, who they can just talk to, or who they can share their story with. Someone who is not out to fix them."[1]

There are so many lonely people in this world and so many gaps in how we relate and "do life" with people. People long for community but don't like how it feels to be placed on a "let me fix you potter's wheel". The newsflash here is that you and I don't have the power to change any one; only God has the power to change people. People need love and empathy, not fix-a-thy.

There's no way you and I can sing on Sundays, "God use me...God send me" and then decide to not be used or sent if the person/people aren't like you. We, those of us which proclaim Jesus as our Lord and Savior, we are the church. We are Christ's ambassadors to the hurting world. God makes His appeal to the world through His imperfect ambassadors, to bridge gaps and build bridges.

There are also many gaps in the hearts of those who have been hurt and had their loved ones hurt by the church people. Many have vowed to never return not just to the building, but also to Jesus. Make no mistake, we will be judged by God one day. Those who chose to judge "certain" neighbors will be judged likewise (Matthew 7:1).

Bridging gaps is not just a job for the "clergy" – it's a job for all Christians. God uses all of His kids to close gaps.

I think about my Grandma Karl. She faithfully prayed every day. This made an impact on me. I pray every day. I'm teaching my kids to pray every day. One person, one relationship, impacted three generations so far.

I used to think one person couldn't really make a difference. But this just isn't true. I think about the one friend who invited me to church where I started my relationship with Jesus. This one person built a bridge to me and it led to my walking over the eternal bridge. This changed my life. Be willing to let God use you to be that one person for someone else, someone who needs to know Christ's love!

As I look through my four decades on this earth, I've seen how God has used one person in many different situations. These "one person" moments added up to many people God used to bridge emotional, spiritual, physical and financial gaps. I've seen a pattern of love bridges built to me. I know (now) it was God who filled those gaps.

As I mentioned, I've seen gaps in my own life. Gaps only Jesus could fill. Intentional gaps left so that I could be sure who was the One who bridged the gap.

When my husband and I went from being DINKs (Double Income No Kids) to being a one income for a family with three people and two dogs, there was a gap in our monthly budget. Every month we withdrew money from our savings account to meet the monthly bills. We knew our savings nest egg would be deleted sooner rather than later. We saw a gap. We didn't stop tithing (giving 10% of our gross income) because of this gap. We took a much more radical approach. We tithed and gave $100 more every month. We asked and trusted God to fill the gap. God may not call you to do what we did, but God will always call you to trust Him and understand He is the one that meets the needs.

God filled the gap, not immediately, but certainly. Months after we gave the $100 above our tithe, my husband's salary increased by 20%. Two years later, my husband earned 100% more than when we gave that first $100. Sure, we worked hard and spent money wisely, but it was God that filled the gap. It was not our hard work; it was our heart work trusting in God to provide and fill the financial gap.

The blessings keep coming. We paid for our last three cars in cash. My friends, I am here to tell you, God fills all kinds of gaps: emotional, spiritual, physical, financial and then some.

The end game of every Jesus follower is not just getting to Heaven, it's to bridge gaps, share Jesus, and bring others with you to Heaven. I know some of this may sound scary because it may seem different. You're free to do and not do anything. There is freedom with Christ. There are rewards for using and consequences for not using your freedom responsibly. Freedom is a responsibility.

Before I received my driver's license, I thought anyone who had car keys had unlimited freedom (and a way better life, too!). But after I got my driver's license, I learned that with freedom comes great responsibility. I still have to pay attention to where I'm going or I could end my life or another's life. I have to spend my money wisely to ensure I have enough money to buy gas. I had to drive carefully (still do) in order to maintain my driving privileges.

Freedom is a responsibility. I am free to build bridges or not build bridges. I'm free to bridge gaps or not bridge gaps. When I was a young girl, I didn't learn a lot about the freedom we have in Jesus. I was told more about God's judgment and rules. So I shied away from exploring my faith because it seemed so rigid. And, a lot of the Christians I met made me feel guilt, a lot of guilt.

If I did five horrible things that day, I felt I needed to do at least six nice ones to be squared away with God. I didn't have a balanced teaching about God's rules (truth) and God's freedom (grace). I had a lot of gaps. And, I saw how I exercised too much freedom with God's rules. I made my faith like a buffet line, picking and choosing what I preferred. And the sad part is a lot of the faith "selections" I put on my plate weren't found in the Bible. But God allowed this. He allows us freedom (Galatians 5:1). He doesn't like it when we abuse our freedoms, just as my earthly father didn't like it when he learned I got (another) speeding ticket. God allows us to make free-willed decisions. He doesn't force anyone into a relationship with Him.

As I look back, I also see how God placed numerous bridge builders in my life. I wasn't ready yet to cross over. I worried if my becoming a Christian meant I'd be/become narrow-minded. I worried about this because I saw some narrow mindedness in a few Christians that I'd met along the way. Then, I completely surrendered my life to Christ. I decided I did not want to be like other Christians; I want to be like Christ. I still have a distance to go, but I no longer go the distance alone. Christ walks with me. The love, acceptance and freedom I have experienced in Christ's love continue to widen my capacity to love, live, forgive, stride and appreciate this life I've so generously been gifted.

It wasn't until I was 20 years old when I decided to walk across the eternal bridge from death to life as I sat in a San Antonio, Texas chapel. The worship enveloped me. I had a personal encounter with the living God. I made another free choice. I crossed the bridge from death to life, I accepted Jesus as my Lord and Savior and now I know after I die, I will be in Heaven with Jesus.

Today, if there's a gap in your life of not knowing if you will go to Heaven, if you don't know Jesus as your friend and Savior, I want to invite you to bridge this gap. This is purely your choice. You're free to say "yes" or "no". I prayed everyone who reads this book says, "Yes."

If you want to know Jesus personally and want to ask Jesus to forgive, help and guide you, but have been injured by the church people, don't let other's shortcomings stop you. Choose to bridge this gap today and remember that Jesus is the only perfect One. I want you to consider praying this prayer right now. The power isn't in the prayer or these typed words. The power is in Jesus. Please say this simple prayer with a full intention in your heart, "Lord Jesus, I have made mistakes which have separated me from you. I don't understand everything about you, but I do want to know you. Please forgive me of my mistakes, help me forgive others, come into my heart and be Lord of my life. Guide me each day. I pray this in your name Jesus. Amen."

If you've prayed this prayer (Romans 10:9), and bridged this gap, I would love to know and celebrate with you. Please let me know at steph@encouragedinheart.org.

I also want to encourage you to pray and look for a Jesus-centered community to grow, give, share, care and invest in. If you're in the Washington, D.C area, you are welcome at my home, The Life Church DC, welovechurch. com. If you're not in the area, you can listen to our nutritious teachings online, which will encourage you as you search out a community that fits you! Just as every shoe doesn't fit your foot, not every church will fit you. Don't let that discourage you! Not pursuing and incorporating into a Jesus-centered community because of the IT gaps is like not going to the gym because of the out of shape people. Don't let human imperfections deter you from bridging into a healthy (not perfect) community and vibrant life!

.*Names changed to protect privacy.

Discussion Questions:

1. Journal/share your thoughts on this chapter.
2. Do you see any gaps in the church community? Where?
3. Do you see any critical or judgmental gaps in your own life? Where? How can you respond differently?
4. Are there any neighbors you could bridge gaps and get to know better? Who?
5. Do you see any bridge building opportunities in these gaps?
6. When have you experienced God fill a gap in your life? What happened? How are you sure it was God?
7. When did you cross the bridge from death to life? Share the people, events and details.
8. Is there an area where you can compromise your method but not your gap bridging message? Where and with who?
9. Are you willing to be a bridge builder? What's your next step?

Chapter 7

GO IS IN THE GOSPEL

*Therefore go and make disciples of all nations,
baptizing them in the name of the Father and
of the Son and of the Holy Spirit. Jesus*
(Matthew 28:19)

I read her email and was not just inspired, I was awed by God's strength evident in her life. My friend *Chris wrote another detailed email about her trip and the precious people she met. A few times a month, Chris and her team go into a Washington, D.C. strip club to befriend the exotic dancers and club owner. I feel like I know many of them because of Chris' emails. I've prayed for the ladies by name. Prayer is a powerful bridge.

Chris and I share a passion to end the atrocity of human trafficking. Human trafficking is the illegal trade of human beings, mainly for the purposes of forced labor, sexual exploitation and slavery. As the world's fastest growing criminal industry, it affects both genders and every nation across the globe. The average age of a trafficking victim is twelve years old. Horrifically, every thirty seconds, someone is forced into this type of bondage — modern day slavery. There are more slaves in the world today than at any other point in human history, with an estimated 27 million in bondage across the globe. Sadly, only 1-2% of victims are rescued.[1]

Many are coerced, sexually exploited, pros- tituted and trafficked through massage parlors and exotic dance venues. Chris won't stand for it. Chris and her team go to the same strip club, armed with a prayer team supporting them, cookies, hugs, open ears and hearts to build love bridges one relationship at a time.

As if this isn't amazing enough, Chris suffers from debilitating Lyme disease. Lyme disease slows Chris down some days, but it does not stop her from living out her God-given purpose. Chris knows she was intentionally created for a purpose, part of which is to end the attrocity of human trafficking.

Chris and her team go to the club with the specific purpose to let the women know that they are loved by the team and by. After months of going into the same dark club, many women are responding. Some are responding by sharing their life story, some with prayer requests, and so far, at least a dozen have left the strip club and "the life".

Christians need to go where people are and realize many will not come to us. We need to go to them. Remember, it's "AND"; we need to extend bridges inside *and* outside the church building walls. The word "go" is in the word gospel.

For years, I sang "GO" worship lyrics in my church, kitchen, sexy minivan and shower. Words like, "Lord use me...Lord send me...there's work to be done in this city...

I give up anything for you...where you go, I'll go." I sang, "Oh yes, Lord I'll go!", but what I really meant was, "just make it familiar, comfortable, safe and also in the local Starbucks. And please, don't let my regular TV viewing schedule be interrupted, either."

True Christ disciples don't just sing worship songs, they say, "Thank you, Lord for your grace and salvation. Send me. I will go wherever you lead me. Use me to help others know you." They go and do likewise (Luke 10:27).

You are made on purpose for a purpose. Every Christian's purpose is to build bridges. The difference rests not in the "go" but in the "how", "who" and "where" you will go. This is different for every person. Our "go" modifies in different life seasons, too.

I was a Hospice volunteer when I found out I was pregnant with Jake. I sat bedside with clients who had just weeks left on earth. What a tremendous honor. I remember one client *Martha, who I brought chocolate to each visit. I wasn't supposed to, but I did. Listen, if I'm in my last weeks on this earth, bring me lots of chocolate and coffee, okay? Okay.

Martha's body and memory failed her. She never remembered my name, but she did remember to look for my hands which carried her chocolate contraband. Martha was delighted to see I was pregnant and faithfully asked each visit if I knew my baby's gender. When I replied, "A boy!" she consistently replied, "Good, because girls are a headache!" What a hoot! She couldn't remember my name or that I was pregnant, but she could remember I brought her chocolate and that girls are headaches!

I was also a mentor to female inmates at Arlington County Detention Facility in Arlington, Virginia. For me to "go" to the women, I needed to ride elevators with unsupervised and unrestrained inmates. There were cameras everywhere, but I knew things could go bad in a moment's notice.

I knew my life was in potential danger before I was pregnant, but after I was pregnant, there were two lives at risk. My husband and I prayed and asked God if I was being irresponsible for potentially risking our unborn child. After three heart wrenching miscarriages, we did not take the baby gift God gave us lightly. So we prayed. God said, "Go!" and I went. There was no way I was going to stop going to that prison just because I was pregnant and a little nervous. I thought about it. Then prayed about it. Got my answer from God and went. When you are inside the will of God, you are in the safest place possible.

A friend shared she thought I was brave to go to the prision and ride the elevators and sit with a group of inmates while pregnant. She couldn't go because she wasn't called to go. Be careful who you take advice from because I could have gotten off track if I compared my calling to her calling. She wasn't meant to "go" where God asked me to go as our "where" and "how" are different. God made us to go to different people and places.

I resigned both of these volunteer positions after Jake was born. Again, I prayed about this. I had peace because God released me from going to both, but not from facilitating a bible study in my hometown. I didn't stop "Go-ing", I adapted to a different season of life and minstry.

I think it's amazing for people to live as missionaries in third world countries because like I said, I prefer the comforts of Starbucks and my

Sleep Number® bed. I could visit a Third World nation, but I do not want to reside there. To me, that's bravery. Chris going into the same strip club, that's bravery. I wasn't called to be her, nor was she called to be me. Use caution and do not compare your mission field with anothers.

I celebrate and am in awe of the way God intentionaly made His kids different. How boring life would be if we were all the same! We all have different talents, but the same purpose to glorify God by loving others. God wants all of His kids to love one another. So if we say we love people but never go to them, "IT" arrives again. People will believe our actions more than our words. If we say we love one another but fail to help a brother or sister in need, IT's not good.

Some people are confused why a group of 20-something year old women would go into a strip club and risk being trafficked. Some might wonder why I'd risk my baby riding a prison elevator. Some may shake their head and wonder why anyone would move to a third-world nation.

You're under no obligation to explain yourself. Don't even try to make people understand your life. Once they see the joy in your life, they will make their own inquiries. Then you have an open opportunity to tell them why you go where you go. Be prepared to give an answer for the source of your "go" and the hope in your heart. But do this with gentleness, respect and a clear conscience (1 Peter 3:15).

When I was a new cop trainee, my instructor trained me to "shoot center mass." This means shoot at and for the heart. Lethal. The heart is the life source. I wasn't trained to shoot at a person's foot to slow them down; I was trained to shoot at a person's heart.

You may be thinking, "Why on earth are you telling me this, Steph?" I want you to remember to "shoot for the heart." As you go where God prompts you to go, I want you to focus on the heart. This sounds so simple. Don't let anything distract you from go-ing for the heart. Not wealth, poverty, tattos, piercings, sameness, differentness, politics. Nothing. We humans tend to look at outward appearances, but God looks far beyond that. God looks at the heart (1 Samuel 16:7).

I shared with my friend that I didn't like the way a particular popular shoe looked. She shared that with every pair purchased, the company donates a pair to the needy. I now think these shoes are absolutely beautiful. My heart changed when I learned about the heart behind those shoes.

I have some beautiful girlfriends that have battled with anorexia. On the outside they are beautiful to me, and looked thin, but on the inside there was a battle unseen to the eye. A battle not unlike my own except I binge while their addiction manifests in starvation. When you meet someone who appears to have the perfect life, avoid the comparison trap. You and I don't know what's going on behind the appearance and closed doors. If you're a Christian, Jesus lives in your heart. Let your heart guide you because your eyes can mislead you. Go for the heart, not just by what you see.

Beloved poet and civil rights activist Maya Angelou wrote, "The desire to reach for the stars is ambitious. The desire to reach hearts is wise." God is concerned with the heart and we need to be also. It's not the outward appearance, it's the heart. It's always been about the heart. Too often, Christians get distracted by the appearances when appearances are often smokescreens for much bigger heart issues.

The whole "love your neighbor" thing, okay commandment, is inclusive rather than exclusive.

We've already discussed the importance of leading with love, but let's be realistic. We are imperfect humans living and building towards fellow imperfect humans.

Realistically, there are some people we will not reach. I think of a person God led me to just this past year. I shot for the heart. I got distracted and shot for the foot but then God refocused my vision and I shot for the heart. I also made and gave soup, turned the other cheek, overlooked some gaps, had a few pleasant and not-so-pleasant conversations and tried. There are some people where bridge construction is delayed and will be continued by another builder. All we can do is go, shoot for the heart, try our best, then rest. Our best is good enough with God, so let it be good enough for you, too.

When you enter into any relationship, remember you're not in the relationship to change them. You're just there to love them. Again, I know this sounds simple, almost too simple. You and I don't have the power to change anyone. Only God has that power. As God changes you and the person you go to, don't get impatient when it appears that you're not making a difference.

When I was a child, we had a large lilac tree in our yard which grew wide and tall throughout my childhood years. The scent and look of lilacs bring back so many wonderful childhood memories. So much so, that after I moved into the first home I owned, I decided I wanted my own vibrant lilac tree. I planted a baby lilac in my back yard. I desperately wanted big lilac blooms so I decided to help it along.

I scooped *handfuls* of fertilizer around my baby lilac. In a few short days, the leaves completely fell off the branches. To say it over-fertilized is a grand understatement. I burned my lilac to the point of no return. I tried to resuscitate with buckets of water, but the damage was done. As I aged and gained some wisdom, I've put *some* of my childish and impatient gardening ways behind me (1 Corinthians 13:11).

I brought the same over-fertilizing mentality to my grassroots approach to share my faith. I think a lot of well-intentioned Christians go in for the kill right away in their eagerness to make people "bloom" with Christ. And, in the over eagerness, we do the opposite. We burn and turn people away from Christians and most importantly, Christ. We're to be bold but sprinkle the spiritual fertilizing nutrition at the right time, God's time. Some people are ready for large and steady doses of God, but in my experience, most are cautious and want/need a slow, steady and consistent feeding. Taking matters into your own hands can be dangerous. Stay close to God and be a patient gardener. Prevent your own burn out by staying fertilized in the Word of God. Allow God to pace you and space the feedings as you serve and feed others. Growth takes time as does trust.

I have a difficult time trusting people right away. Trust takes time to build. As you go and become trustworthy, share both your strengths and weaknesses and allow others the same freedom. I guarantee that when you authentically present an accurate picture of yourself, reveal your heart and allow another the same opportunity, change will happen for both of you.

As you go, keep your relationship with God the top priority because we need God to direct and lead us. So many times in our eager attempt to both introduce others to Christ and train disciples, we take matters into your own hands and over fertilize. Give the God-directed amount; any more or less then that will prohibit proper growth.

We must go beyond just introducing others to Christ and calling it a day; we're to make disciples that will replicate the "go" work of Christ. David Platt captured the disciple making process so beautifully in his book, *Radical*, "Making disciples is not an easy process. It is trying. It is messy. It is slow, tedious, even painful at times. It is all these things because it is relational."

The disciple making process is relational. God wants us first and foremost in a relationship with Him. God gives us our family (biological and spiritual) to grow and know God more. It's in relationships with God and others where we are all changed. As our vertical relationship with God matures, we change for the better, which improves our horizontal relationship here on earth.

You have many natural relationships in your family, home, community, job, school, church and places where you live your life. Often times, God doesn't call you to "go" to the furthest ends of the earth. He wants you to "go" to work or your grocery store with a bigger purpose than your job or week's groceries. Some of the most powerful God bridging experiences occur when and where we go and carry on with our normal daily life, like in a grocery store, our job, a bookstore or in a doctor's waiting room. God brings the people we're to meet and build relationships with and to.

There are also some intentional relationships where we need to go. You'll know you might be getting close when you see a group of people where your heart aches. This heart ache is called passion. Pray about what makes your heart ache to carry out your passion by living out your bridge-building purpose. Prayer and community will help you identify and understand your God-given passion. If starving children makes your heart ache, you have intentional bridges to build. This may mean participating in a local food drive or going where you're unfamiliar or uncomfortable like in a third world nation.

It's important we build bridges both where we have natural relationships as well as building intentional bridges where you lack natural relationships; like Chris going into the strip club. Wherever God puts a burden on your heart, pray and go there. God put a burden on Chris' heart for human trafficking victims and she goes. If reading this last paragraph stirs something up inside you, stop reading, start praying and listening for God's direction.

There are some people you have natural relationships with where you may not realize you need to go. After I became a Christian, I abandoned many of my before Christ (BC) friends. These friends should never be forgotten. Why? Because there's a natural relationship built with a sturdy love foundation poured and trust established.

I want to rest here with the BC friends because I've seen people like me, who have crossed the Great Bridge and behaved like I did. They turned their backs on their old life (good) and old friends (bad) under the well-intentioned notion of holiness.

First of all, there's nothing I can do to be holy outside of God because God is the originator of holiness (1 Samuel 2:2). We're holy because of Who we love (God). We can let go of sins and some bad habits but again, we need His power. This is only possible by God's holy power in us. God's people are set apart by God (2 Kings 4:9) to go and do God's work. We're set apart to go and be used by God for God's purposes. We're set apart, but not set away from, others.

If you and I choose to live in a high holy tower set apart from humans and surrounded by our own "holiness," how do we live out the command to go and make disciples while in isolation? Remember your old life friends were once you before you crossed the Great Bridge. As you share the joy and hope you have, your loved friend might consider crossing the Great Bridge for them! At the very least, they will get to know about Jesus better as you love them more like Jesus does.

I want to recognize the need and wisdom to separate from old destructive BC life patterns. There needs to be a time where you separate so you can leave behind the destructive patterns, habits, sins and possibly the people that could lead you to stumble back into those patterns (Galatians 6:1). So guard your heart, but don't isolate it. God chose you, called you holy and dearly loved (Colossians 3:12).

I believe I very possibly could have made fewer bad choices in my younger years if someone came into the bars I sat in and cared to share the good news of Jesus. I'm so incredibly proud of Chris and her team for courageously going where they continue to faithfully go. It takes time to build trust. They are making a difference. They are building friendships and eternal bridges.

When and if you need courage, study where and how Jesus lived. Jesus shot for the heart with adulterers, lepers, tax collectors, religious folks (Pharisees), and fisherman that He met in His everyday life. This is the Jesus model of "GO". It involves having interpersonal relationships with different people in your everyday life.

There was a time when God called me to go somewhere very, very different. I prayed and asked a dozen close and trusted friends to pray. God said, "Go!" and I made all the arrangements to go. It cost a lot of money, time, energy, effort and faith. Ego too. After all the details were in place, I still wrestled with going. Two times I woke from sleeping in fear. I reached out to the same prayer friends, because my courage was wilting. My ego is very, very big and I feared what others would think of me, almost more then what God thought of me. Ego (pride) is a very slippery slope if left unchecked. God asked me to go and let go of my ego, which was Easing God Out. Don't let your ego ever Ease God Out. I held my realistic and humanistic fears up to the following questions:

~ How far would I go to reach non-Christians?

~ Would I risk comfort?

~ Would I risk money?

~ Would I risk reputation?

~ How far would I go to reach someone for the Gospel's sake?

~ Is there someone I wouldn't try to reach?

Then, I substituted "Jesus" in for "I" and re-read the questions.

~ How far would Jesus go to reach non-Christians?

~ Would Jesus risk comfort?

~ Would Jesus risk money?

~ Would Jesus risk reputation?

~ How far would Jesus go to reach someone for the Gospel's sake?

~ Is there someone Jesus wouldn't try to reach?

Jesus gave me courage and friends to help give me courage. I did go. God wanted me to physically travel alone, but I didn't *really* travel alone. God and my prayer friends traveled with me. People's opinions are getting less important.

I would rather be found exceptionally flawed doing something good for God than be found absolutely perfect sitting on the sidelines doing nothing for God. I don't want to stay in the locker room or the sidelines; I want to get in the game!

Maybe something ahead of you feels "BIG". Ask God to help you respond in faith, not react in fear. Worship God, not your emotions. Encourage yourself by reading the above questions and don't let others or your ego, Ease God Out!

When you go and meet people who reject your God message – shake it off (Matthew 10:14). I know it hurts and is challenging to not take personally. Keep going; keep sharing and planting God's love and message. There will be a harvest (Galatians 6:9).

We live in a broken world, but must reject and prevent the broken world's ways from being adopted as our own (John 17:15-19). As you prayerfully go build bridges in the world, allow God to utilize your past for someone else's future.

Back when I was a cop, I was selected for a short-term undercover assignment with a small team. Our mission was to go identify and incorporate into groups, who bought, used and sold illegal drugs to military members.

Our team was diverse. It became quickly clear all but one team member had some experience in a "party lifestyle" because of how effectively they fit into our target areas. One of our team members was so nice but never partied before, which is awesome for her, but not for our mission. It was painfully transparent as she tried too hard and "over fertilized" and burned some of our efforts. She was too eager. There are only two kinds of people who are eager to get information about drugs, cops and addicts. She didn't look or behave like an addict so this left one option. You see, she didn't have the life experience to know how to relate with the people we were intentionally sent to relate to.

Some things in life are bad, but God can use *all things* (Romans 8:28). Yes, even my drunk party years can be used for good. I use this example to encourage you regardless of what your past is, trust God can make it good for you and for others! I'm not saying "go undercover" with your faith or the Gospel, I'm saying use your past for someone else's future to advance the Gospel! There's nothing God can't leverage for good if you let Him because your life and story matter.

God wants to use your past, present and future for good in His story.

Don't be ashamed of who you were or who you are. You're not trusting others with your story, you're trusting God! There's no shame as you share your former pain for God's gain!

Share your story boldly for God's glory at the right moments. Your past isn't useless. In fact, it's useful in sharing who God is in your life. Just as scars are proof of a physical healing, sharing your story is proof of an emotional healing and sharing about your God in your scar story is proof of spiritual healing. Shoot from your heart for another heart and go build a bridge!

Thanks for spending this time together reading about building bridges. Now, GO! Here's your official invitation to the GO PARTY:

WHO: Me

WHAT: Build bridges

WHERE: Everywhere

WHEN: Now

WHY: To bring God glory!

No RSVP needed, just go!

Remember, God loves you and wants you to GO:

- keep calm and build a bridge
- love, not judge, others
- acknowledge other's pain
- serve inside and outside the church building
- apologize
- bridge gaps
- go live out your unique purpose!

Our goal is not to build a bridge just to get over it; our goal is to build a bridge to get to it; the work of reaching the precious hearts that need to hear that God loves them and cares for them, today. So go, build a love bridge, and tell them the Good News.

I believe these beautiful words by Mother Teresa will encourage you as you go about building bridges.

> "If you are kind, people may accuse you of selfish, ulterior motives: Be kind anyway.
>
> If you are successful, you will win some false friends and true enemies: Succeed anyway.
>
> If you are honest and frank, people will try to cheat you: Be honest anyway.
>
> What you spend years building, someone could destroy overnight: Build anyway.
>
> If you find serenity and happiness, they may be jealous of you: Be happy anyway.
>
> The good you do today, will often be forgotten by tomorrow: Do good anyway.
>
> Give the world the best you have, and it may never be enough: Give your best anyway."[2]

Jesus didn't die for you and me so that we can live a boring, unfulfilled, pre-packaged just like everyone else kind of life. God made you on purpose with a unique mission. God didn't make you to be like everyone else; He made you to be YOU! Be boldly you. It will encourage those around you to go and do likewise!

*Names changed to protect privacy.

Discussion Questions:

1. Journal/share your thoughts on this chapter.
2. Make a list identifying where you have natural relationships. Where do you see any bridge building opportunities?
3. Are there places where God wants you to build an intentional bridge? Where?
4. Have you isolated yourself from your BC people? This may be good and this may be bad. Evaluate and share.
5. Have you ever considered yourself a missionary?
6. Do you believe it's the heart that's most important to God? Why or why not?
7. Has there been a time when someone bridged to you and solely focused on your heart? When? Recall what was meaningful to you.
8. Have you ever gotten distracted from heart issues because of someone's differences? What were the specific differences?
9. Is there a person or a group of people where you find yourself challenged to shoot for the heart?

ADDITIONAL RESOURCES FOR FURTHER BRIDGE BUILDING READING:

Love is a Verb: Stories of What Happens When Love Comes Alive by Gary Chapman

The 5 Habits of Highly Missional People by Michael Frost

Love Does by Bob Goff

The Forgotten Ways – Reactivating the Missional Church by Alan Hirsch

The Faith of Leap: Embracing a Theology of Risk, Adventure and Courage by Michael Frost and Alan Hirsch

Untamed by Alan Hirsch and Deborah Hirsch

The Prodigal God by Tim Keller

Blue Like Jazz: Nonreligious Thoughts on Christian Spirituality by Donald Miller

Radical by David Platt

Redeeming Love by Francine Rivers

The Jesus I Never Knew by Philip Yancey

NOTES

Chapter 1 – Keep Calm and Build a Bridge
1. Alan and Debra Hirsch, *Untamed* (Grand Rapids: Baker Books, 2010), 77

Chapter 2 – If Only I Knew Then, What I Know Now
1. Smith, August 21, 2013(3:08 PM), "Judge Judy is highest-paid TV star," *CNN Money*, http://money.cnn.com/2013/08/21/news/companies/tv-guide-judge-judy/
2. Rick Warren, Twitter, January 18, 2014 (12:44pm), https://twitter.com/RickWarren/status/424598083939217408
3. Henshaw, Stanley K., and Kathryn Kost, August 2008, "Trends in the characteristics of women obtaining abortions, 1974 to 2004," *Guttmacher Institute*, on line [http://www.guttmacher.org/pubs/2008/09/18/Report_Trends_Women_Obtaining_Abortions.pdf].
4. "Bible Gateway," John 8:7, New International Version. http://www.biblegateway.com/passage/?search=John+8%3A7&version=NIV

Chapter 3 – Lead With Love
1. "How to Adapt," Mission Frontiers, July 1, 2012. https://www.missionfrontiers.org/issue/article/how-to-adapt

Chapter 4 – In AND Out

1. "Preaching What We Practice and Talking the Walk," Bringing TRUTH.com accessed June 16, 2014, http://bringingtruth.com/OtherStuff/PreachingWhatWePracticeandTalkingTheWalk.aspx

2. Alan Hirsch, *The Forgotten Ways* (Grand Rapids: Brazos Press, 2006), 285.

3."Love Your Neighbor As Yourself," Christian Bible Reference Site accessed June 16, 2014, http://www.christianbiblereference.org/jneighbr.htm

Chapter 5 – Unleashed

1. *Halley's Bible Handbook*. Grand Rapids: Zondervan, 1965). 442

Chapter 6 – The Gap

1. David Schimke, "Finding Yourself in a Crowd" *Experience Life*, May 2014. http://experiencelife.com/article/finding-yourself-in-a-crowd/

Chapter 7 – Go

1. "The Facts," The A21 Campaign, content accessed June 16,2014. http://www.thea21campaign.org/content/the-facts/gjekag

2. "Mother Teresa Quotes" Goodreades.com, content accessed June 16, 2014. http://www.goodreads.com/author/quotes/838305.Mother_Teresa?page=2

Steph Fink is an inspirational communicator who encourages hearts to live out their unique God-given purpose. She lives in Virginia with her husband, Dave, two children Caleb and Jacob, and their dog, Crash. They have a grown, adopted-by-heart child, Jayson, that lives in Arizona. She is a proud partner with The A21 Campaign to end human trafficking. Visit her online at encouragedinheart.org.

To inquire about having Steph speak at your event, visit encouragedinheart.org for a menu of her speaking topics or email contact@encouragedinheart.org.

Steph would love to connect with you at:
FaceBook: Encouraged in Heart
Twitter: @StephanieFink
Instagram: @encouragedinheart
Pinterest: encouragedinheart

Encouraged in Heart
PO Box 231413
Centreville, VA 20120

CPSIA information can be obtained at www.ICGtesting.com
Printed in the USA
BVOW07s0807110914

366322BV00001B/1/P